Contents

My inspiration from Kimron Corion

I remember receiving a message via Facebook from a young lady indicating that she had a story to share using our platform #IamGrenadian. Although she wanted to let others know about her experience, she was nervous about sharing. Her uneasiness stemmed from the possibility of a poor reaction, hostile reception, and unrelenting backlash by society towards her, since her story dealt with the abuse she received as a child by someone she looked up to and loved. Nevertheless, I encouraged her to speak out because I believe that sexual abuse and incest are topics that have been on the backburner in our society for too long. Someone needed to let everyone know about that distasteful situation that plagues our society, and I am glad she did. After she shared her heartfelt story, the response she received was overwhelming. The support from the entire Grenadian community, both locally and abroad, was so great that it started a movement and conversation around sexual abuse and incest and ultimately led to the book you are about to read.

Sexual abuse is unwanted sexual activity that is forced upon someone without his or her consent. It can be in the form of unwanted touching to forced intercourse. Traditionally, sexual abuse has been mainly mentioned in relation to females. However, males can also be victims of such abuse. Unfortunately, recent reports show that there has been an increase in the abuse

of minors of both genders by guardians, teachers, and even family members not only in Grenada but across the world as a whole. Sexually abused victims normally exhibit a number of unusual behaviours like withdrawing from society, refusing to eat, mood swings and temper tantrums, sudden fear for certain people or places, nightmares, or having trouble sleeping. Therefore, parents need to be very vigilant and look for changes in their children's behavioural patterns. Additionally, parents need to have a watchful eye on their children because the lack of parental support can further add to the agony that abused victims endure.

One reason why Michelle was reluctant about sharing her experience was that society often tends to judge and berate the victims. In many cases, they have been called liars especially when the accused is someone others admire. Such unfortunate situations should never be the case. Sadly, Michelle knows about the backlash all too well because as you will see in her story, she didn't receive much support when she attempted to reach out to others and talk about what was happening to her. Consequently, if a child indicates that he or she is being abused, take the complaint seriously and never make any judgements about the child. Instead, remain calm, thank him or her for sharing, promptly report the incident once there is a shred of legitimacy, and let the child know that the abuse is not his or her fault. Even most importantly, children should always be encouraged to speak openly about what happens to them, just like Michelle who eventually opened up and received the support she needed.

This book talks about one girl's journey from victim to survivor, from being sexually abused to becoming an advocate and activist for victims of sexual abuse. Her story shows that with the proper support one can overcome anything. As you read this book, remember that Michelle's unpleasant past is the present for many unfortunate individuals. Therefore, focus on the

broader picture, the impact of sexual abuse on the victims. No longer should the taboo nature of sexual abuse continue to hide in the crevices of society. Instead, the unsavoury acts should be lamented, brought to the fore, and alleviated.

Kimron Corion
Co-Founder - #IamGrenadian

Preface

"You better keep quiet eh," he commanded, as he penetrated me with his fingers, moving them around in a circular motion, with each movement followed by scorching pain.

Being abused is a traumatic experience that no one should face, especially children. It affects them everyday, and the abuse leaves scars that take a lifetime to heal.

Many people fail to see into the lives of these victims of abuse, the social, mental, physical and in some instances spiritual hardships that they often encounter. *Helpless Cries* was written not only as a result of my personal experiences as a survivor of sexual abuse, but also because of the increase in the prevalence of abuse against young children in the Caribbean and around the world.

As I began to write, I thought about the personal nature of the information and began to question whether people would be interested in reading the private and agonizing recount of my experiences and the stigma often attached to victims like me.

More than that, this book also exposes the failing systems of our institutions designed to protect and the silence of our citizens. It tells the story of a child who had her innocence brutally stolen, and who was confronted by her fears, the fear of her abuser, and the abuse itself.

The account follows the transition of an average child into one that is troubled, abandoned, victimized and re-victimized; a hopeless child, lacking confidence; a child who cried for help, but to no avail; a child who was failed not only by those she loved, but also by the systems of society.

The purpose of the book is to break the silence and stigma surrounding sexual abuse and to educate the public on how they can be greater advocates for victims. As a people, a nation and a society, we all have a part to play in curbing this issue.

This book will help you understand that sexual abuse is not a taboo, but a troubling issue that calls for our undivided attention.

Sexual abuse is everyone's business and must be treated as such, especially for the children who cannot protect themselves, and need society to help them fight for their rights.

Every broken child forms the reflection of a broken society.

It is time that we play our roles in looking for the signs, and to act, thus removing the cloak of silence. As the old adage says: *It takes a community to raise a child*. Let us become that community for this generation and those tomorrow.

Note from one of the Editors

Aptly named.

This was the thought running through my mind while editing this text. This was a challenging and emotional task to complete. I alternated between heartbreak, blinding rage and sadness for Michelle and with them, a feeling of helplessness that there was nothing I could do to help. My heart broke time and time again, for Michelle and all the other Michelles after every betrayal; physically by the accused who are supposed to protect but who preyed and emotionally by parent, school and community that often has more empathy for the accused than the victim. The re-traumatization and judgement in the court of public opinion hurt me to the core.

But Michelle is a survivor and I am honoured to have been given this opportunity to do my part for her and young girls and boys like her. I could feel her trauma, pain and desperation, all the way through. I kept wishing that there could be a happy ending. Unfortunately in the story there wasn't, until now, until this text, written in local parlance and with gut wrenching familiarity, which speaks to the context of poverty which often precludes or has a role to play in stories of abuse.

My wish is that through this narrative all those who have been victimized will find the courage to speak out like Michelle did. Here I would like to commend my business partner and co-founder of iamgrenadian.com, Kimron, who first encouraged Michelle to share her story on our Facebook page. Her sharing took incredible courage and I am so glad that for once she got the support and empathy she deserved. I only wish that more survivors like Michelle would have more encouragement, support and safe spaces to turn to. Kudos to her for embarking on this journey to ensure that others who may fall victim to this type of abuse will find the support, resources and appropriate judicial recourse to heal the wounds inflicted.

Congratulations on your first book!

In solidarity,

Trisha Mitchell-Darius

Toronto

Reviews

The book, *Helpless Cries*, by Michelle S. Alexander, is a must read for anyone concerned with child abuse or has experienced abuse.

Child abuse is any injury that is intentionally inflicted on a child by a caregiver. Common forms of abuse among children are neglect, physical assault, emotional abuse and sexual assault.

Sexual assault is widely recognized as the most lasting form of abuse. Victims of sexual assault often grow up with emotional, work and relationship problems long into adulthood.

Helpless Cries is about rare courage—an innocent 10 yr old beauty that had four years of her life stolen away by a trusting family member. It's a very vivid, insightful and graphic tale inside the mind of a girl who refused to let her frightening and troubled past stop her from becoming a proud productive member of society.

She is determined to get the signs of abuse out to the public and raise awareness for care and concern to the victims who she can relate to oh so well.

Read *Helpless Cries* from start to finish through the eyes of one brave, big hearted, forgiving, Christian girl who grows up to be a person we all can be proud of.

Thomas Murray, USA

This book, *Helpless Cries*, takes you on a vivid journey and shines light into the silenced darkness of a child who was sexually, mentally, physically and emotionally abused by one whom she trusted to protect her. Instead she was chastised, ridiculed and stereotyped by those who considered this a "taboo subject" to talk about, shunned by those too scared to speak out against the abusive monster and by peers and others who simply didn't, couldn't or refuse to believe or understand.

As a reader, the actual fear and pain through the chapters, turn like a dagger in your heart, setting off a raging anger within you at her "monster"

and all those who failed to protect her innocence and her virginity—
something she will never be able to give (her virginity) to the man of her
dreams because he has ripped it away.

No amount of showers or scented baths can erase his smell or wash that
scar away. Now the silence and helpless cries of this sexually abused child
is broken and heard through this book, thus encouraging silent sufferers to
take that step forward and break the silence.

Beverly Adams

Acknowledgements

Firstly, I would like to thank the Lord for giving me the strength to survive such a traumatic ordeal. Without His divine intervention, I would not be here today to share my testimony.

To the two men who played a paramount fatherly role in my life—Michael Noel and Bernard Joseph—words are not enough to express how thankful I am towards you both.

To my brother Devon Asthon, and my little sister Meisha Alexander—thanks for always standing at my side and believing in me.

Cindy Doyle, I thank you kindly for all that you have done for me over the years.

To Miss Rholda Quamina—I cannot find words to express my gratitude; you made me much of what I am today.

To the Teacher of Bishops College, I thank you.

I extend a heartfelt thank you to Kenita Henry, Kimron Corion, Sherry Robertson and Kenroy Baptiste.

Thanks to Trisha Darius for being one of the editors of the manuscript and Mia Belfon for doing the cover design.

Mr Dubai Campbell—thanks for taking the time to proofread the manuscript and thanks for your positive words of encouragement.

Special thanks to Ms Rehanna Warren—your support has been greatly appreciated; you have given so much of your time during this journey.

Michelle Belfon who read almost every chapter and provided positive feedback, Correen George, Kimron Corrion who supported the idea of a book from day one. Rosalie walker, Paulette Thompson, My WAS sisters, members of GCSCORED as well as the Heal With Hope foundation.

I am grateful to all those who contributed to the publication of this book. I would also like to thank the following persons: Hon. Delma Thomas, Sandra Johnson, Ashook Abdool, Nordia Roberts, Mr Claude Douglas, Mr Tevin Andrews, Mr Joel Greenidge, Mr Andre Donald, Dr Nadine Isaac and my colleagues from the Ministry of Social Development and Housing.

To my publisher, Rocima Publishing—your hard work did not go unnoticed.

To Tony Urbansmash from Overcome Foundation for bringing this eBook edition to Amazon Kindle.

Special thanks to the Grenadian public for your unwavering support. To my mother and other members of my family, I thank you kindly.

Chapter 1: Ring Games

Who is going around pansy,
Hello little fellow,
Who is going around pansy.
Hello little girl,
So what can you do pansy,
Hello little fellow,
What can you do pansy.
Hello little girl.

I in the ring and I running around as they sing, I put my hand on my waist and wine around, and they started singing again.

So we can do it to pansy, and everybody danced; they hand on they waist too. Elisa looked a little bit awkward because she has two left legs, but she doesn't mind because she dancing too.

So who will you choose pansy,
Hello little fellow,
Who will you choose pansy,
Hello little fellow.

I whirled around the ring thinking about who to choose; Tasha looked at me and I knew what the look meant. She wanted me to choose her so it could be her turn to dance in the ring. The sun was setting and the street lights were going to be turned on at any time. I touched Tasha and she went into the ring. We all sang again and Tasha made some silly tricks; she stretched out her tongue, bent her back like an old woman and shook her foot. We in turn stretched out our tongues, bent our backs and shook our feet. We laughed too because Tasha was looking like an old granny and we were playing granny too. Everyone had a turn in the ring, and then we all sat down in the road close to the standpipe thinking of another game to play.

Whenever it was playing time I was always excited. Everyone came together like a family; it was always a great togetherness and sometimes we told jokes. Tasha always ended up peeing on herself with laughter. Tasha laughed at everything and her contagious laughter sometimes had me laughing too.

"Allu oye, what we playing next?" Crista asked, taking out her slipper to crush a congaree that was taking its merry time strolling up the road. I hated congarees, especially the small ones. Dey does go in your ears, travel to your brain, and kill you—well so dey say.

"Let's tell some scary stories!" Dedra shouted.

"Nah, I 'fraid and outside getting dark; ah 'fraid, ah want to sleep tonight."

"Allu! Allu look ah jumbie!" Tasha shouted jumping up from the road as if she really saw a jumbie, and I jumped up too. Tasha started laughing again.

"Sabrina way you running to go, you think you could run from spirit?"

Tasha was joking but I was serious. My heart was beating so fast and I always got goose bumps whenever anyone spoke about jumbies.

"Ok, ok, let's tell some jokes or Anansi stories."

"Jokes?" Crista asked.

"Who telling the joke?" Tasha asked, "Cuz I run out."

"Me," Ricardo said. "Ah have a joke."

We all gathered closer to listen to the joke.

Ricardo ent even start the joke yet but Tasha laughing already and rolling on the ground, the gravel filled earth digging into her skin.

"So there was three people on a plane: a Grenadian, a Trinidadian and a Jamaican. The plane was about to crash and dey was asked to throw five dollars outside and say: *lord save me*. So the Grenadian throw a five dollar bill, he say, 'lord save me' and a parachute appeared and he was saved. The Trinidadian did the same thing—he throw he five dollars, say 'lord save me' and he was saved, so the Jamaican was the only one left. He search he pocket but he din have change so he throw out ah ten dollar bill. The parachute come, he watch it and he ent take it."

"And what happen?" I asked, anxious to know what happened next.

"Hush you mouth let the boy finish nah," Elisa exclaimed, as if she in a rage. I remained quiet and listened.

"So the plane crash and the Jamaican ended up in heaven. When he reach now, God ask him, "But why you never take the parachute?" He answered, "I was waiting for me change."

Tasha was the first to laugh and everyone else laughed too. That was a good joke, but that Jamaican was really silly—he waiting for his change.

"Who going to tell the next joke?"

"Nah let's do some riddles."

We all agreed.

"What goes up and never come down?" Ricardo asked.

"Smoke."

"Wrong!"

"Then what?" I asked.

"Somebody else turn to guess!" Ricardo said, frowning a little.

"Your age." Elisa remarked.

"Correct."

"Okay, okay my turn."

"Ah making chairs, ah doh want it; ah give somebody and they doh want it—what am I?"

Everyone was scratching their heads trying to figure out the answer.

"Coffin," Donelle shouted.

"Yeah you correct." I had told Donelle that riddle already.

We played some other ring games and told each other stories, laughing our guts off, until it was time for us to go inside. It was getting late and although it was safe to be outside in the dead of the night, we had to go home at a reasonable hour. We skipped happily down the road, walking with our backs turned so that whatever jumbie following us will stay outside and we will have a peaceful night rest, without the jumbies trying to hold us down.

Chapter 2: Anxiously Awaiting Uncle Jack

It was early in the morning. I ran around the yard, only partly dressed. My

jersey felt heavier and heavier as I continued making circles around the

house. The wet mud stuck between my toes; some had even splashed on top

my campesh bone. The rain water hit my head, but it did not sound the same

way it did when it hit the roof—it made little water marks on my skin the

same way it makes water marks on the callallo leaf in the drain that Mama does cut on Sundays to make "baggi."

"Sabrena, get your backside out ah the rain!" Mama called from inside.

"Ah coming Mama, ah bathing." The rain was falling heavier now and I was getting cold bumps, but I was not ready to go inside. The water felt cool on my skin and it made my hair feel cosy.

"You better wash your hair one time eh miss woman," Mama shouted again.

"Pass the blue soap for me."

I stopped right in front the house and took the blue soap from my younger sister while she looked at me with her two cokey eyes. I wondered if it was me she was watching. I rubbed the soap in my hair until it formed foams and then I ran around the house again. The soapy water ran down my face, burning my eyes. I was having fun and wishing the rain will go on pouring forever.

"Rain, rain go away, little children want to play," I sang, not really wanting the rain to stop.

"Sabrena, Sabrena." Mama shouted. I stopped and ran inside the house, pushing the wooden door open. The water dripping down my body, the same way it does fall down from the galvanise. I run straight inside, the water dripping on the floor, making a long trail. I know if Mama called my name one more time I was going to be punished.

"So Sabrena you can't wipe you skin?" Elisa asked shoving a piece of coconut in her mouth. I stuck my tongue out at her and grabbed a big jersey from the corner of the floor, drying the water off my skin.

I looked around the living room and everyone was sitting on the floor. Elisa and Dedra were sitting in the corner playing 'country, boy, girl' while Troy was leaning against the wooden partition sucking his tongue with his mind like it in space. I know if it was not for the rain Troy would not have been home so maybe that's what was on his mind, with his dreevay self. Donelle and Jim were fighting as usual.

"Move out ah me space Jim," Donelle shouted.

"But Donelle you bold oui that's my space."

"You space in the cemetery boi, move nah."

I watched them and passed straight because, dem is bam bam and pork and I did not want to get tangled up in their business. Mama lay down on her bed eating coconut husk mixed with sugar. The mosquito coils burned to keep away the sand flies that were waiting for the rain to start falling, so that they can start their invasion, stinging people hard, hard, hard as if you do them something.

The atmosphere around the house was light; we were not cursing or tugging at each other as we used to. And it was not because of the rain that was falling nonstop. We were all excited because it was the day before Uncle Jack, our new stepfather, was to join our household. Mama was speaking about it regularly and reminding us to be on our best behaviour and not make her shame. I had an image of Uncle Jack in my mind based on Mama's description of him, but I had never seen him before.

I finished drying my skin and grabbed a top from the barrel—a green top that belonged to my sister. But that was not a problem because we were used to wearing each other's clothes and sometimes we even wore each other's panties.

I looked around the hall for a comfortable place to sit down. The rain was still falling heavy, but all the corners were occupied, so I went to the bedroom and threw myself on the sponge—the sponge that I shared with my other siblings that always left pieces of foam in our hair. I was in a good mood, beyond excitement, to meet Uncle Jack since I had heard so much about him.

"Sabrena."

"Yes Mama?" I answered. The rain was making me dozy, especially with all the running I did.

"You dry your hair?"

"Yes." I lied because I knew if I only said No, Mama was going to cut me backside.

"Come let me feel it."

"But Mama, it dry; it just have a little bit ah water."

"If you dry it, how it have ah little bit ah water, come here."

I picked up myself, feeling tired as if I had run a marathon, and pushed myself through the board where the little piece of partition was missing, busting out into Mama's room. I pushed myself below the wire that Mama used for hanging up clothes and a pants brushed across my face, the button almost blinding my eyes.

"Oh gosh," I cursed in my mind, "What if that stupid thing did blind me; it think it have eyes selling in store?" Steups!

"Come here gyal." I walked up to Mama while she was still chewing her coconut husk. I looked at the window covered with mist from the rain and the little rain flies flying around. I had an urge to kill every one of them, but that was impossible. Mama had called me and I had to give her my full attention.

"Come let me feel that hair of yours."

I walked to the edge of the bed and Mama rubbed her hands through my damp hair.

"Sabrena, that dry?" I did not answer.

"Sabrena is you ah talking to. Ah thought you say you hair dry eh, is me you want to be running in Mirabeau Hospital tonight behind you? Ah tired tell you it cheaper to bury you than to mind you you kno, so if you want to play stupid with your life go ahead, because when you can't breathe is right there I leaving you. You know how it does be with you and that asthma ah ready. Go and get a cloth and come here before I lace some belt behind you back. Is like you looking for a warm up in this cold weather."

I walked towards Mama's barrel and pulled an old piece of cloth which I gave to her. Mama rubbed the cloth in my head until it was dry.

"Get out in front of me," she said. When she was finished, I walked back through the piece ah partition and into our room.

This rain was looking like if it had no intention of stopping, so I crawled below the dirty sheets and covered myself from head to toe. I heard a thunder roll and I closed my eyes expecting lightning but this time it did not flash. I closed my eyes shut, forcing myself to sleep.

"Sabrena wake up. Food." Just the name of food was enough to wake me from my deep sleep. I jumped up from the bed and stretched my body. Darkness was already was creeping through the room. I could see the faint candlelight in the living room.

"But Sabrena, ah thought you was sleeping eh?" Dedra asked.

"Doh mind her you know, is greedy she greedy; just the name food and she jump up from she bed ah ready; ah sure if was to go to school all the shake you shake her she ent waking," Elisa chipped in.

"Allu leave the girl nah," Troy said, while his double row teeth were showing as he grinned at me.

"Sabrena you is me real girl come on eat ouii"

I made myself comfortable on the floor and my belly roared with hunger. My mouth watered at the smell of the coconut bakes and stew back and neck, wondering why Mama was taking so much time to hand me my bowl.

"But wey me food," I asked with dribble running down the side ah me mouth. I was no longer sleepy; all I wanted now was to eat, belch and go back to sleep, and anxiously wait for the arrival of my new uncle.

Mama handed me my food and I ate greedily; the back and neck melted in my mouth leaving a taste that sent an urge within me to beg for more, but I knew the consequences of begging. I left my plate on the counter, making the little I got sufficient. I rinsed my mouth and went straight back in the bedroom, for I wanted the space at the corner before anyone else had taken it.

I lay down thinking about how happy it was being a child, unlike my older sisters. Life was nice for me—no clothes to wash, no house to clean and hardly any chores to do.

"Sabrena, Sabrena," Dedra called from the living room, "Why you never wash you plate?"

I sucked my teeth. Steups.

Wash which plate? Wah she talking bout?

"Mama say ah can't wash wares."

"What you mean Mama say you can't wash wares. Mama, you tell Sabrena that?"

Mama answered confirming what I had just said and Dedra grumbled under her breath. I was too far away to hear what she was saying, but I did not care. My eyes were growing weary once more so I just shut them and waited for sleep.

Chapter 3: Uncle Jack

The day had finally arrived. We were all up early to welcome Uncle Jack.

We were happy to have him and we hoped that he was the one to make a

positive contribution towards our standard of living and quality of life. My

mother had constantly reminded me of how helpful he was towards her when

she was pregnant and she and my father had fallen out. I had great love for

my father, but I always had a spot in my heart for that man that my mother spoke so much about. They had had a relationship in the past, so "the old fire

stick catch back." Being told how he was there for me, I had a special love

for him.

My first reaction when seeing him was to express my gratitude and to let him know how thankful I was of him to play such an important role in my life knowing fully well that I was another man's child.

Uncle Jack seemed nice, and he was funny too! He told us real nice jokes, and he brought us gifts from prison. He brought some real nice fibre glass rings and a chain. Prison in Grenada is like a learning centre; they teach you how to make nice things. They teach academics too. People say you could go in dunce and come out bright, bright; brighter than the mid-sun. Some people say it is a five star hotel and people go up there for vacation because its life in paradise; you doh have to worry about nothing—no bills to pay and three square meals a day.

I got a matching Selassie-I set and you should see the smile on mi face. Ah was well happy because he brought me something nice. Uncle Jack sat down and made himself at home, giving us the joke about Miss Celina. We sat down on the floor and we were attentive—if ah pin drop you hearing it. We eyes in he mouth like we wanted to eat the words.

"Papa, Miss Celina hear everybody doing hair and Miss Celina want to do hair too, so she dress up and go by the hair dresser. On her way, she met Mr Rabbit. Curious to know way Miss Celina going with comb and straightener, Mr Rabbit asked the question. Mr Rabbit coulda dead when Miss Celina say she going and do she hair, because is two grain ah hair Miss Celina have on she head; it could only twist because its literally two." We burst out laughing, rolling on the floor because the joke sweet and we know somebody quite similar to Miss Celina. And so the rest of the day went with Uncle Jack, all where he was I right in he footstool because I love my stepfather too bad.

Not two good days yet and Mama and she prince charming start cursing already; she telling him to go by he family and she don't want him in she place, how he is ah jailbird and she should have left him way he was. Is like Mama have curse and it bothers me whenever she start to cuss I does feel real sad. I does just go in a corner and pray that things go back to a peaceful state, because I could not understand why a big woman have to carry on like that.

But Uncle Jack not answering; he was ignoring her, and that was making her more furious. She hand on she waist and she cawaying she head,

"Is you I talking to macco. Don't ignore me in the place me father dead and leave for me."

I felt sorry for him, but I feel more pity for Mama. I couldn't help thinking that when I grow up I wanted to be different. I want to have one boyfriend and we must get married. We will build a nice house and make some pretty children and we not cursing every minute. And my husband must have a nice job, dressed in jacket and tie and ah nice van just as Mr Mark. Not like Mr Ben—he van does sound like ah old truck and it does break down all about in the road and he always have to have water; is like he vehicle does overheat. But Mr Mark have a nice ride. It does sound light when it going up the hill and inside it nice and comfortable. I know because I get a ride with him ah few times.

So Uncle Jack and Mama still vex and I trying to console Uncle Jack. Ah telling him doh study Mama, she go come around. He say I should not worry; he know me mother and what he dealing with, but I still feeling sorry for him. I don't think he deserve that kind of treatment because he is ah nice man. But like he know better so I leave him and went under the cocoa to see how much mango fall. My sister asked me if I think me eyes ripening the mango because I just come out under the tree and ah going back. But I did not have time for Elisa, ah going and see if it have mango under the tree.

Chapter 4: Betrayed

Five months later...

It was sometime in the month of May—the date I can't precisely remember

—but things at home were going a lot better. Uncle Jack does iron our clothes

and he does cook too. Sometimes before he go to work early in the morning,

he would get up and make bakes and if he have time he would make callaloo

fish cake. Uncle Jack was the first person I saw making fish cake with

callaloo but it does taste nice and ah liked it. He does always put a big piece on me plate and sometimes I does get more fish cake than Elisa and them,

and dey so greedy they does watch me plate and quarrel. They say Uncle Jack

like me the most because he does treat me the best. Even when he come out

from work and he bring fruits he does give me my share first.

I really liked Uncle Jack; I couldn't wait to heave myself on his lap and hug him tight around his neck. Sometimes he does smell like sweat but I doh care, I hugging him still.

Sometimes Uncle Jack does hide and give me an extra twenty-five cents for school too and he does tell me buy a lolly or something nice. I don't really like sweeties so I does save it and after school, buy a cocoa snow ice by Miss Justina.

One day Mama asked me to accompany Uncle Jack to the garden and I was overjoyed and excited. Other than liking outdoor activities, I know that the garden was loaded with cane and other fruits which I loved passionately. My other siblings were afraid of the bush; they were conscious about they skin being bruised and them getting galay, although most of them skin was done galay ah ready.

I grabbed my boots, got my fine bag, collected my cutlass and waited for him. It was rather a quiet walk towards the garden. I stopped part of the way to pick up and inspect the mangoes that had fallen on the ground. The sun was rather hot and no one was on the road as we made our journey. At last we reached the garden.

"Sabrena."

"Yes Uncle Jack." I bent down and was picking up the nutmeg that had fallen on the ground, pelting them in the paint bucket and making a loud noise.

"Can you do me a favour?" He asked.

"Yes," I replied.

"You sure?" I was still picking up the nutmeg, with my back bent and I inspecting them to make sure them that did not have mace still good because some of them does be growing and when you bring them in the pool they does throw them away.

"Yes," I replied once more.

He was now walking towards me; his big shoulders printing in the stained shirt he had on. He reached close to me and he stopped. I stopped too and I looked up at him with a big smile on my face wondering what it is he wanted me to do, because I ain't mind doing anything for him.

"Boom me!" I felt my heart sink. I looked at him and then I looked at the paint bucket in me hand. I looked at him again wondering if I was I hearing right.

Boom him? His request had shaken me somewhat. I knew his demand was wrong and there was no way in which I was going to agree. My heart beat in my chest and I grew nervous and frightened at the same time. Boom was the colloquial term for sexual intercourse.

"No!" I said, "No, I can't do something like that; besides you are my father!" I was looking up in the tree as if it was going to tell him no too.

He walked closer towards me with the cutlass in his hands; it took all the courage I had to keep me from crying, and from running too. It was hard to explain what was going through my mind; it had to be a dream because there was no way the man I loved so much, the man I adored, the man I respected, obeyed and looked up to was actually asking that I have sexual intercourse with him.

"You will Sabrena and that is a command."

"I won't Uncle Jack, I won't." It was at that moment I tried running but he swiftly pulled me back. My heart in me toe; I was literally shaking, frightened and bewildered.

He grabbed my jersey and I tried pulling it away. The same way I use to pull away and leave the jersey in Mama's hand when she want to beat me. I was shaking like a leaf and my foot started feeling weak, as if I go fall down any minute.

I looked at him as he walked away from me relieved, then he stopped, turned back and my heart went down in my toe. He was walking back towards me again with the cutlass in his hand.

"Come here," he ordered. I walked towards him without hesitation, trying not to upset him. I was afraid he would change his mind and boom me.

"Sabrena this is our secret; the minute your mother or Blackboy hear of it, you will be sorry. Any word or any sign of what happen here today, you will be sorry for you self. Doh say ah ent warn you, and Patsy will help me kill you!" Patsy was the correct name of my mother.

I just stood there, rooted as if I was one of the nutmeg trees and frightened as if I had seen a ghost. Uncle Jack walked away. I sat down below the tree and buried my head in my hand until it was time to go home.

Chapter 5: Mama Break Hand

Mama and Uncle Jack does still curse and fight, but this time Mama make

him go and he living down the road by Mr Ben. I happy because he not there

to watch me funny and I feeling a little safer. After he had asked me to have

sex with him I did not want to be close to him anymore. I don't run and heave

myself on him again and I don't hug him up either. I try and keep to myself.

Mama sent me in the shop to trust a pound of flour and some back and neck. As I was walking back up the hill, (Plaisance big hill that does make you feel tired, as if you come out and run a marathon), ah see Donelle running down the road.

"Donelle what happen, how you running so?" I asked.

Donelle is my younger sister and they say we look alike. She small, small like she don't want to grow, but she bright and she could run fast too (not faster than me doh; I fast like lightning). She tried to talk, but she was out of breath so I waited till she catch she breath.

"Mama and Uncle Jack cursing and dey want to fight."

I looked at Donelle; she look so frightened and fragile.

"What they cursing for?"

"Ah doh know Sabrena, but Mama down the road by Mr Ben and she telling Uncle Jack she go kill him."

Ah wanted to tell Donelle that's not my business, because I did not know why she ran down the road to tell me that for; why she did not run and go Grenville in the Police Station. But I cared about her too much and the look on her face had me feeling sorry for her.

"Let's go up eh girl. Look a Bourbon biscuit. Eat it fast before we reach home. I thief out ah the money Mama have in she bag to buy the Bourbon biscuit that have the nice chocolate in the center. I wanted to buy ah penacool too but not me and the woman money; I had to thief with care."

Donelle grabbed the biscuit from me and opened it. She looked up, smiled at me and I raised my hand playfully to hit her. No doubt about it, she is my favourite sister and we have a strong bond. I like her more than all my other sisters.

As we bend the corner by Mr Frank, ah hear Mama loud basket mouth.

"Macco man, come out from around here. Come out around meh father place and go. What happen, the house you stinking dirty mother dead and leave down town it have lion and tiger in it?"

"Doh torment me Patsy. Quite wey I dey down here you coming to harass me? I out ah you place. Leave me alone." Uncle Jack talking at the top of his voice and he mouth echoing. I sure the people in De Blandeau could hear him.

"Ah want you out ah Plasiance you panty full macco. Go! Go!"

I continued walking up the hill. When I reached Mr Ben gap, ah slow down. Mama was still cursing. Uncle Jack leave wey he dey and he start walking down towards her. He had an evil look on his face; the same look he had when he threatened to kill me if I tell Mama anything.

Why Mama don't leave the man and go? Why she come all down the road to harass him? I watch Donelle and she shaking as a leaf; she eyes full up ah water and it's like she want to cry. I doh like to see people crying. I know if

Donelle cry I will cry too.

Uncle Jack got closer to Mama and she ain't moving; she have she hand on she waist and she watching the piece ah wood on the ground, letting him know she doh fraid him. Mama like to fight and Mama did go in jail before. She did take a banganet to kill Mr Zack and he brought her up in court. Mama feel she bad because she say she know what the prison life is like and she not afraid to go up dey and spend ah little holiday.

"Patsy I tell you leave me alone you know." Uncle Jack went up in Mama face.

"What you go do macco?"

Mama push him and Uncle Jack almost fell. Thank God for the bank he braced himself on.

Uncle Jack leaned forward and he eyes full ah rage. He grabbed Mama by she neck and he threw her down on the ground.

"Go up Donelle," I shouted.

"No, ah not going anyway." I don't really want Donelle to see the commotion because I know how soft she is.

Uncle Jack was on top of Mama. He pressed his foot on she chest and she trying to push him off.

"Get up on me Jack, because if you ain't kill me now, you won't like what go happen to you."

Mama pushed again and this time she got him off from on top her. She turned around and at the same time picked up a big stone. Uncle Jack get up and he grab onto a piece ah spice wood. As soon as Mama go to raise she hand, Uncle Jack pull back he hand then he hit her one lash on she hand. Mama screamed and the same time the stone drop from she hand.

I closed my eyes as if it was me feeling the blow.

"Oh God, oh God me hand break!" Ah never hear Mama bawl before but she was bawling now and ah wondered how she know she hand break.

"Let me see it!" Uncle Jack said and he grab she hand. Mama did not pull away she just let him look at it. Like dey ain't want to kill each other again.

"It break in truth; you go have to go in the hospital."

Uncle Jack went into the house and return with ah piece of cloth. He tied the both ends and put the cloth over Mama head.

"Put you hand in that; let me see if I get something to drop you in the hospital."

He hurried up the road not even worrying to put something on his feet. Five minutes later he returned with Mr Thompson. Uncle Jack was sitting in the front seat of the vehicle. He stepped out and opened the door for Mama. I just stood there watching the vehicle going round the corner and out of my sight. For the first time in my life I wished I had a weapon to damage Uncle Jack.

My mother was a beautiful woman, in her late thirties, almost six feet tall, with long black "dougla" hair, smooth skin, a long face, straight nose, brown eyes and the most lovely cheek bones I had ever seen. People complimented her on her beauty, but most disliked her ways.

She was a straightforward woman, who came across seemingly disrespectful, warlike, quarrelsome and defensive. Villagers feared the sound of her name and few tried never to cross path with any of her children. Since she fought like a man and cursed like a mental patient, most persons considered her mad anyway. She told people the things she knew about them, what she thought she knew about them, and even what she thought will happen with them in the future. Yes her mouth was bad. After receiving a verbal wiping from her, villagers would make themselves scarce for very long periods because of the embarrassment and them being the centre of gossip, based on allegations and secrets, most of which were not true as revealed by my mother.

Most of my siblings including myself had different fathers. So yes, she was promiscuous. I'm not sure if it was because of her vulnerable position, since she was poor and had to make ends meet, which is something men took advantage of.

At age sixteen she had already given birth to my elder sister and sadly had to become a single parent since my sister's father had three other women pregnant at the same time. The revelation only became clear to her after she had given birth. His role in her and my sister's life after that was quite marginal. My mother therefore had to fend for herself with little support and assistance from her upset and regretful parents, whose hope was on her to lift the family name and make them proud. Their hopes were dashed when she got pregnant.

She had denied herself a sound education, the major vehicle to climb the stratification ladder and go upward ending the curse of poverty that existed in the family generation. So she herself had fallen as a victim of poverty. My other two siblings followed in quick succession, being only one year apart. Then I was conceived almost 21 months after the tragic death of my grand father, who whilst trimming a tree fell with his chainsaw, cutting him open and leading to his instant death. To my belief and calculation I was conceived sometime in March 1991, since she gave birth to me on the first of November the same year.

Chapter 6: Defiling My Trust

Mama and Uncle Jack returned later with her hands in a cast and a sling

around her neck to support her broken arm. They were no longer quarrelling.

He was now comforting her and letting her know how sorry he was for what

he had done. It was something I always struggled to understand—one minute

they both wanted to kill each other and the next moment they were good

again. But it was rather difficult to comprehend—maybe that was the way adults reacted to each other.

"Allu eat ah ready?" Mama asked as she made herself comfortable on the house step, pushing aside our slippers that occupied the whole space.

"Pasty, ah going for my clothes," Uncle Jack said, not even giving any of us the chance to answer our mother.

"Ah right," she replied. I was in shock. I turned to look at my siblings wondering if they had heard the same thing but they all seemed not to be interested.

Uncle Jack was going for his clothes to bring it back home! But why? After all he had done! After he had left her to care for a broken arm! I got up from the step and walked towards the room. Earlier I was hungry, but now that I realised that monster of a man was returning, I was no longer hungry.

It was clear my mother was out of her mind and here I was feeling sorry for her, wishing I was old enough to protect her. The scene played over in my mind—the way he had her pinned to the ground, her screams and how she cried. Something was indeed wrong with her accepting him back. Maybe she was afraid of him.

I felt my chest tightened and I prayed it was not another asthma attack.

"Sabrena," Mama called.

I pretended not to hear and continued walking, Mama had indeed upset my spirit so answering her was now the last thing on my mind.

"Sabrena yuh doh hear ah call you?"

I had now reached the door to the bedroom and turning myself around I answered.

"What you want Mama?" I asked, trying to hide the anger from my voice.

"Who you asking what dey want? Go in the room and reach the soft candle for me, let me rub my fingers."

I walked into her room, searching through the shelf. I found the white and red bottle with the red writing that said, *Soft Candle*. I collected it and walked back towards her, dropping it in the lap of her skirt.

"Sabrena come closer to me. Is you chest that wheezing dey?"

I walked closer towards her and she leaned her head to my chest, the same way we sometimes lean our heads towards the radio when the batteries are weak and it was almost impossible to hear anything.

"Hmm, yuh chest wheezing in truth. You and this asthma, and more I tell u about the dust and water you won't hear. Go and lay down let me send Elisa to get some bush to boil for you."

She instructed Elisa to get the bush. Just as I was about to enter back into the house, I spotted Uncle Jack breaking the corner of the gap and walking into the yard. I turned my head quickly to avoid his gaze and walked back towards the bedroom. I heard my mother and the rest of them speaking but I covered my ears since I did not want to hear any of them.

I was still laying on the bed when my sister returned with the hot cup of tea.

"Drink," she instructed and all to eh; we going down the road by Aunty May. Mama say you should stay with Uncle Jack since you not well.

"But why?" I asked. "Why can't I come? Why must I be the one to stay home?"

"Sabrena but you sick. You have to stay home."

"I don't want to. Its my chest and not my foot; ah could walk."

"Mama say you not coming. You know her word is final. You drink the bush and just keep yourself quiet."

"But ent Mama hand break? Wey she going with break hand?"

"Why u doh go and ask her?"

I steups at Elisa and drank from the cup; the hot tea stung my lips and the bitter taste took over my taste buds.

"Any way Sabrena, we going. Uncle Jack dey if you want anything."

I knew better than to suck my teeth for my elder sister, so I cursed in my mind as I looked at her walking out, leaving her scent of rosemarie and camphor behind.

I was still in the room when I saw the shadow hovering over me. I looked up and met the cold gaze of Uncle Jack. He was standing and leaning against the upright board that that supported the patition.

"So you mother say you sick?" He was the first to start a conversation.

"Yes," I murmured.

"Well no one ent dey home—just the both us. Your mother asked that I take care you, so ah guess we go boom tonight."

My chest wheezed and this time I was able to hear it—he had started making his advances again, the same thing he had done in the garden.

"Boom who?" I asked.

"You," he replied, "And this time I'm not asking you; I'm telling u."

I was still laying down on the bed in our room. I looked up and he was walking towards me. My first intuition was to jump through the back door, but it was closed and he was already walking towards me.

"No!" I shouted as he approached me.

The word had barely escaped my lips and the next thing I knew I was in his arms with his hands over my mouth and heading towards my mother's bedroom.

I felt the pain tearing through my stomach as a knife making its way through the body of a cunning animal. I kicked my feet and shouted at the top of my lungs, but not a sound escaped my lips. His hands covered my mouth, sealing my lips, stifling any sound. Pulling my legs apart, his rough hands circled my vagina. Within the split of a second I felt his fingers trying to force its way inside me. The pain was unbearable. I was a virgin; my body was not capable of handling this kind of attack. I jerked my body trying to break away from his touch, but it motivated him to push further and as he did I felt a gush of pain running through my body. It was sharp, so sharp that I wrenched violently. He was a man almost four times my age, with big firm, hardened fingers. I had never felt such pain in my entire lifetime, nor had I imagined my vagina would hurt this much.

"You better keep quiet," he demanded as he penetrated me with his fingers, moving them around in a circular motion with each movement followed by a scorching pain. My heart wrenched and tears flooded down my cheeks. I could not believe this was happening; he was a monster. He paused, and I opened my eyes hoping it was over. Was it the end? To my dismay it had only just begun. He began pulling down his pants and reaching for his private. I had no intention of seeing his nakedness so I shut my eyes at first then looked to the corner of the bedroom, blurred by tears. I felt his hands grabbing my chin.

"Look at me!" he shouted.

I remained reluctant because I had no desire to see his manhood. If he was really going to rape me then he might as well hurry and get it over with.

"Look at me; kiss-meh-assing me!" he repeated.

There was sharp anger in his voice and I obeyed instantly. He was caressing himself, rubbing his hands over his penis. He stared at me straight in the eyes sending chills all over my body. Never in my life had I seen the nakedness of a man; his penis, scared me. I was afraid.

"This Sabrena, is for yuh." He was now shaking himself.

"I longed for this moment. From today onwards it is yours. I will have you whenever I want, whereever I want and as long as I want to, and you dare not say anything to your mother. Besides she will never believe you. We all know she hates you; she hates the best bone in you. You know you are not one of her favourite child. She'll never take your word over mines. But just in case you decide to try it, ah going back wey ah came from and this time it will be for murder."

I knew very well what he was saying. Before joining our household he was released from prison where he had spent the last two years of his life. Reinforcing his threats, he squeezed forcefully at my throat.

"This is our secret Sabrena no one must hear of it."

I cried bitterly from within. It was clear that my mother hated me. I tried to understand what was going on, but nothing was making sense to me.

Why was he hurting me? Was it a game that adults played with children? Inside, my soul wept bitterly. I had looked up to Uncle Jack, respected him, trusted him and loved him like a father, whilst in return he did nothing but orchestrated a plan to hurt me, to take away my pride and destroy my innocence, and to break that trust and respect I had for him. If only it was possible for him to choke on his words—wicked monster.

Without waiting for a reply he continued, "You can make this easy by relaxing, or you can galavant to cause yourself pain. I know it's your first time and I promise to be gentle. I promise to take my time and I also promise that I'll do anything to ensure you enjoy it."

Was he mad? Was there anything to enjoy in being raped?. My mind grappled to understand what was happening. Was there anything on me to have him sexually excited? I had no pubic hair, no breast, no hips, nothing. What could he have seen in me to want to do this to me? I was just a child.

Never in my life had I imagine something like this. He was the last person I thought would hurt me. As I felt his weight on my body, I shut my eyes once more, tighter this time.

It was dark except for the shadow of the moon, that cast her shadows through the windows, creeping through the galvanise, giving a faint light to the room. The crickets were singing as usual. The sounds they made normally irritated me but tonight I was finding comfort in them; they were sort of keeping my mind off the tragedy. For the very first time in my life I wanted them to sing louder.

I heard the barking of a dog as I breathed in the mixed scent of sweat and coconut oil from Uncle Jack. If only it was possible to move my hands then maybe I could have tried pushing him away, but he had me pinned down in such a way that I was motionless. I squeezed my eyes even tighter, thinking that the pain will go away, trying to pretend it was only a dream and block everything out of my mind. But the pain was too much to dismiss; impossible to ignore.

By now he was gyrating on me, slamming his heavy frame against my small body, penetrating deep down inside me. Each gyration was accompanied by pain. This pain seemed not only physical, but mental and emotional.

It was at that moment I started questioning myself. Why was I left with this monster? How could he have done that to me? Why did he have to make me feel so miserable? But I had no answer. It was too difficult for me to understand. I felt a part of me crying bitterly from within. If only the pain will go away or at least end!

I started praying and hoping for a miracle. Then I heard him moan. It was a sound of pleasure. Before long I felt his hands on my throat pushing me against the cold headboard. As his body increased in motion, the tears continued flowing down my cheeks. Thrusting further, harder, deeper and gyrating once more. I shifted my body trying to ease the pain which made it even more unbearable.

I wished the house would come crumbling down and the earth will welcome me into her surface. There were no words to express my true feelings. I felt as if my soul had departed from my body; even worse, tangled up in the deep forest, amongst the strongest ropes.

I fought effortlessly to push him away but my strength was nothing compared to his heavy weight and body mass which left me vulnerable. As if celebrating my defeat, he eased himself up and looked at me with a cruel smile on his face. I was trying not to look at him, by keeping my eyes shut. But I wanted to see his expression and to my disgust he seemed all excited and satisfied.

That heartless monster! I had trusted it with my body, soul and mind. To make matters even worse, he seemed so proud and delighted with himself, looking as if he had accomplished his life goal.

For the first time in my life I felt naked, empty, betrayed, robbed and even neglected. Where was God when I needed him the most? Where was my mother, the woman who had vowed to protect me, who carried me in her womb for nine long months and saw me through ten years of my life?

Where were my guardian angels? Was Christ only a myth? Does He care about His children who are innocent, helpless, needy and even defenceless? God must surely help me through this I thought, as I whispered a short word of prayer. As if hearing my supplications I felt his weight lifted off my body.

"I hope you enjoyed it," he whispered in a tone which sounded cold and deadly. "I also trust you won't tell anyone about this," he whispered again while his heavy frame was still on my scrawny body.

He did not wait for a response but continued, "Even if you do Sabrena, no one will believe you and let me tell you why. Your mother is not too fond of you; you are not one of her favourite children. She hates you and will never believe your word over mines, so I'm telling you, please don't waste your time. Remember, it's our little secret."

He continued, "Just one word, one sign, one indication and I will be forced to return to that that place where I came from and this time it will be for murder. So the minute you lose your consciousness and allow it to slip from your lips you will be as good as dead."

I shivered at his threat. Something within told me he was serious and that

I should proceed from henceforth with utmost caution. It was his words that pierced through my heart, causing me to shiver. It was true that my mother disliked me and it was even clear to him since he had it all figured out, properly orchestrated. Hence the reason he had targeted me instead of my other sisters. He had even waited for the right moment when no one was at home. I hated him. God, I hated my mother even more.

His hands gripped my throat and he squeezed tightly indicating to me that his threats were true. So many thoughts raced through my head. Was he serious? how could I have enjoyed being raped? How was I supposed to enjoy my step father having sex with me? He had to be insane. Why in God's earth did my mother befriend this monster? Why did she allow herself to be married to such a creature?

He eased himself up, his naked body in full view. Trying hard not to look at him, I turned my head in the opposite direction.

"Look at me!" he shouted. But I could not budge; my body was too heavy. I felt weak.

"I said look at me Sabrena!" I could hear the anger in his voice.

I forced myself to turn, opening my eyes and looked at him. He was staring at me straight into my brown eyes holding his penis in his left hand.

I felt angry and ashamed looking at him, but I was more angry and ashamed of myself. Hell, he had just robbed my entire childhood and I was defenceless, unable to protect myself from this evil. Pulling up his pants he then left the room and urged me to clean up myself.

Chapter 7: Bloody Scene

I covered my face, with my eyes remaining tightly shut. I listened as his

footstep made an impact on the wooden floor. I heard the click as he opened

the door and the sound of the loose stairs as he descended and went outside.

Once he was out of earshot, I buried my face in my hands and cried bitterly, trying hard to ignore the pain I felt. But I soon realised that I had better start cleaning up since crying was not going to solve any of my problems. The deed was already done.

I tried pulling myself together, but the pain was so intense that I had no other choice than to lie on my back and remain immobile. It was at that moment that the negative thoughts started consuming me, taking over my mind. For the very first time in my life I felt naked, useless, unwanted, rejected, empty and used. I even went as far as contemplating suicide. After all, there was nothing much to live for. He had already taken away the one thing that meant so much to me.

I clearly remember a pastor once saying: *A woman's virginity is a gift from God; hence it is important that she keeps and preserves it for the honourable hour. It was only to be given to her husband since it forms a covenant between man and wife.* What was I to give?

To my dismay, his discharge was all over my stomach. Between my thighs felt sticky and as I examined myself I realised that I was bleeding heavily. The coat he had placed beneath me was soaked with blood. With trembling hands I reached for a cloth and started cleaning myself.

His discharge smelt fresh and was cream in colour. It was becoming stickier as I wiped at it trying hard to shut my mind away from the tragedy. I rubbed the cloth against my leg in an effort to wipe away the blood stains.

I did not hear him return, but I felt when he grabbed the cloth from my hands and ordered me to open my legs.I was reluctant. He then pulled my legs apart and wiped my vagina. He was rough and I wrenched in pain, but he ignored me and continued. As soon as he was through, he picked up the soiled cloth, dirty clothing and my undergarment, demanded that I took my bath and then left the room.

I attempted to stand up. I was partly naked, but weakness overcame me and I lay back on the mattress. I was wearing a top which was cut just above my navel; it was one of the many pieces of clothing I had outgrown which left me practically naked from the waist down.

I looked around slowly. I was in the room he shared with my mother. He had raped me on his matrimonial bed; well, his matrimonial mattress since there were no beds in our home. Compared to our neighbours, we were relatively, in fact chronically poor.

Even the room was empty, except for a barrel in the far corner where my mother kept her clothing, and a hand built shelf in which she stored her toiletries and other items. There were two windows—one facing the road and the other looking down to the lands we refer to as being "under the cocoa."

At last I mustered enough strength to rise. As I stood, I felt a gush of warm thick substance flowing down my legs. Gingerly I forced myself to walk towards the shelf. I felt for the lamp, collected the matches and lit the wick which gave light to the small room.There was blood everywhere even though my attacker did some cleaning. I felt my knees go weak and I fell straight on to the floor.

Chapter 8: Daybreak

The next morning broke with the usual howling of the dogs, the crowing of

the roosters and noise in the atmosphere. But something within me felt

different; it was a usual morning but I was not my usual self. In fact I was

never going to be the same and there was no denial to that.

To my surprise the room was cleaned and my bloody clothes removed. I was cleaned up and lying on my bed. Guess Uncle Jack had done all these things after realising that I was knocked out cold.

He had removed all the evidence. The only thing that was left was the pain in my heart and burning sensation between my thighs—the pain I was about to face every day of my life. Oh my, at age ten I was already no longer a virgin.

I hated him more than I hated any other thing in the world. He was not deserving of my love and I had no more love for him. He took advantage of my trust, love, kindness and weakness. He was not just wicked but cold hearted while he pretended that he loved and cared for me.

I felt lost, rejected, unwanted, hated, unloved, cold hearted and betrayed. I was still in a daze when I heard my mother's voice summoning me to the kitchen. I removed the bed spread and walked slowly towards the hall, parting the stained blinds. I walked into the kitchen area where my breakfast was served in the corner of the floor.

Unlike other families we had little or no luxury. No fancy chairs; in fact there were no chairs at all except for the car seat in the far corner of the sitting room that my elder brother occupied as his bed. There was no flush toilet, television, running water or telephone. The fireside was our cooking area in which we all took turn, fetching firewood.

Most people looked down on us because we were relatively poor and the constant pregnancy of my mother with hardly anything new unless a donation was given by the church or someone in the community who pitied our situation and felt sorry us.

I was walking into the kitchen with a limp, but no one had seemed to observe. I was even walking slower because I was still feeling the scorching pain. To my dismay my stepfather was seated on the floor in the far corner with my mother. He was busy talking but I blocked my mind off him, since I had little or no intention of hearing his voice.

I walked in and sat on the floor, just next to my younger sister.

"Sabrena, who the hell is your companion; can't you say good morning?" It was the voice of my mother—angry and aggressive as usual. I pretended not to hear as I made myself comfortable staring around, looking at nothing in particular, trying to get the horrific experience of last night's activity out of my mind.

"Patsy, I find Sabrena getting really out of hand. Imagine you talking to her and up to now she ent answering, I don't know how this child coming out so."

It was my stepfather of course. I had no idea what he was trying to do, but whatever it was, it was getting me angry. I wanted to stand up and shout out exactly what he had done to me, but I remembered his threat so I kept calm, waiting for my mother to pass her remarks or punish me, because I knew it was not yet over.

"Ah tired tell this little black wretch, nobody inside here is her companion and two female crab cannot live in the same hole, and when I say ah doh like her allu does want to talk. Ah doh know why the ass I din make a tub ah ice cream instead of making this little good-for-nothing child eh. The ice cream woulda finish ah ready or maybe ah should have left she ass in the hospital. Ah does wonder you know if you is me blasted child. You better start looking for your mother." Mama's words cut deep within.

I had no idea when I started crying, but the slap across my face broke my trance and brought me back to reality. She was now furious and shouting.

"You want something to cry? Take this!" My mother was raining slaps across my face and my stepfather was there supporting her, urging her to continue and reinforcing the need for me to be corrected and disciplined. Bloody hypocrite!

"Eat!" she demanded as I sobbed quietly.

I had no appetite for the bake and bush tea before me, so I played with it a little and when no one was looking I pushed it in the direction of my brother who welcomed the gesture and smiled.

Chapter 9: Aftermath—Munich School

I reached for the bucket behind the house, picked it up and walked towards

the stand pipe that was just in front our house. I did not fill it to the brim

since I knew it was going to be difficult to carry. In the state I was in, there

was no denying, that I was feeling weak and helpless.

It took me almost ten minutes to carry the water to the backyard; a task which usually took less than a sixty seconds. I looked for a spot where I would not be visible, took my clothing off, reached for the soap and dipper and poured the water on my skin. We had no bathroom; so bathing outside and paying attention to our surroundings was our only option.

As soon as the water came into contact with my lower body, my vagina tingled and pained once more. I bit my lips to avoid screaming.

After my shower, I made the necessary preparations for school and began the thirty minutes journey not saying a word to anybody.

The school was located in Munich and there was no form of transportation to get there from where we lived, so our only option was to travel by foot; something we had grown accustomed to.

I decided to walk all by myself since I was in no mood to entertain company. The usual thirty minutes, turned into two and a half hours in which I cried silently every step of the way. When I arrived the class was already in progress.

Miss Thaxle stood at the board, lecturing the Math lesson. Everyone was busy writing and trying to solve mathematical problems. With my hands on my forehead I greeted the class; all eyes were fixed on me.

I felt my knee buckled and once again I grew weak. Late coming was not acceptable, no matter the excuse and at that point I had no excuse whatsoever to give.

I stood at the door staring awkwardly at the teacher; she had dropped her hands from the board and was now staring at me with her hands on her hips. I glimpsed at Aliah, my best friend, sitting at the far corner of the classroom; she looked very concerned. I knew she was scared for me.

It was there and then I had a leap of courage. To hell with what Ms.Thaxle had to say. I was in no mood to entertain her foolishness. Besides, it was my class and I had every reason to be in it.

Adjusting my bag strap I stormed into the classroom. Everyone stopped in unison and all eyes were fixed on me.

"And where do you think you are going, Miss Sabrena?" Miss Thaxle asked.

"In my seat of course!" I shouted.

My response had taken her somewhat aback, for she stood there for almost one minute staring at me. I felt no remorse; no regrets. With eyes fixed on her I continued walking. I could see the muscles in her face began to tighten and somewhere deep within I felt a sense of satisfaction.

"Get out Sabrena!" she shouted

"I'm going nowhere!" I shouted back at her at the top of my lungs with anger enveloping my voice. "This is my class and I belong here." I continued, "If I must go then give me back my school fees."

"I said get out!" she repeated.

"And I said I'm not going anywhere!" I reinforced.

She ignored me and walked towards the table, rumbling through her desk packed with papers. She reached for the straps, which indicated one thing. I was about to be punished, at least that's what she thought, but there was no way I was going to allow her to raise her hands on me, not after what I was forced to go through last night.

I turned myself around where I could have direct eye contact with her. She was walking towards me almost eight feet away; her shoe heels making crackling sounds.

"You best know what you doing with that straps!" I shouted. "Because you won't like it if you touch me," I continued.

She continued walking towards me and the next thing I felt was the sting of the strap across my back. I yelled in pain and frustration, grabbing the strap, pushing her against the wall. We both held onto the strap; me tugging on the left and her tugging on the right. I felt like slamming her against the board, knocking her head against the wall and knocking her out of consciousness.

The rage from my stepfather did to me was directed towards her and the monster within me was coming to life. By then there was a loud commotion. The teacher from Grade Five had come across to separate us and demanded that I follow them both to the principal's office.

The principal's office was located downstairs at the two storey building just opposite the kitchen. Mrs. Patrick was the principal. She was nice, but strict. She had a belt that most students believed she soaked in stale pee that made the impact of the blows harder.

But who the hell was Mr. Andrews to tell me to follow him to the principal's office? I was going nowhere; if he wanted me to go he was going to have to drag me. Something he dared not do. I looked at them both with anger and frustration written all over me.

"Sabrena, the principal office I say!"

"I don't want to see the principal; if you think she should see me then maybe you should invite her to come."

My classmates were now laughing, increasing the noise and commotion and it was evident that Sir was getting upset.

"For the last time Sabrena, the principal office!"

"Are your forcing me?" I asked, "I said I'm not going anywhere! Do whatever you have to do. But just don't put your filthy hands on me, because you won't like the end of the story."

I had made up my mind. I was not going anywhere. The only place I was moving to was my seat; nowhere else and that was final.

They both stood there looking at each other trying hard to decide what their next move was going to be. I remained rooted in my spot staring back at them.

"Don't forsake a whole class for this Jezebel," he said to Miss Thaxle. "There are actually children who woke up this morning and came from good homes with the intention of coming here to learn."

What was he trying to say? Was he insinuating that I came from a bad home and learning was not my interest? Lawd Jesus, that fat stinking man called me Jezebel. I wanted to tell him who is Jezebel or where he could look to find her but at the same time the bell rang. It was lunch time.

Chapter 10: Flashbacks

I wish I had somewhere else to go than home because I did not want to face

Uncle Jack. It was the worst day of my life and the worst school day I ever

had.

Before, when the school bell rang for lunch, I used to be excited to go in the pasture where I played running games with my friends, after we ate our lunches from the tuck shop. But today I just wanted to be left alone.

"What happen to you Sabrena?" Aliah asked.

"Nothing," I replied as I shook my head at her. There was no need telling her, because she was never going to understand and besides I couldn't tell her. Uncle Jack had warned me against telling anybody and I was afraid of dying.

"You vex about what Miss Thaxle do?" Aliah asked.

"No girl, I doh even have Thaxle to study."

"Then what happen, why you doh want to play with me? Its lunch time lets go for our lunch. Today is bakes and chicken."

I always liked when they cooked bakes and fried chicken but today I was not eager. I was not busy to run down the stairs like I used to, pushing my way to reach fast in the kitchen.

"Ah doh hungry Ali; go ahead nah."

Aliah looked at me with her big eyes and I could see sadness in the corner of them.

"Go gyal, go, I ent feeling well, ah sorry."

She opened her mouth to say something; she glanced at me then turn around,

"Ah coming back, ah going for me lunch and I eating right here."

I watched as Aliah walked out the class room. The breeze blew her skirt and she pulled it down quickly, looking around to make sure no boys saw her blue tights.

The boys in our class real forward; they would put mirrors in their shoes pretending they are talking to you while watching under your skirt. Especially Ron—only mischief he does study. Ron older than us because he stayed down. He stayed down and he still dunce. He knows nothing that's going on in the class. But when it comes to trouble he is the ring leader. They don't practice they stupidness with me because I could fight and I don't make them stupid jokes. Once Ron hit me and after school when we were passing in the back road, I beat him up and make him eat mud. Since after that me and Ron is best ah friend. He don't grandcharge around me; he know what tree to climb.

I put my head in my hands on the table and I closed my eyes. But I seeing Uncle Jack and I still feeling his weight on my body. Ah hearing his voice in my head and smelling the scent on his sweaty body. Its like Uncle Jack right next to me and it feeling as if he raping me again.

"Sabrena wake up!" Ah hear Aliah voice and I feel she hand tapping me on my shoulder.

"Aye girl ah ent sleeping," I looked up and she have two plates in her hand, smiling down at me.

"Ah bring lunch, for you. Eat, you might feel better."

Ah did not want to make Aliah feel bad so I take the food from her hand. The red bowl have a cut on the side and a black spot on it, looking as if it make its time and it need to be thrown away from the kitchen.

"Thanks Ali."

I played with the food. I really was not in the mood to eat, but at the same time I don't want her to feel bad so I just bite ah little piece ah the chicken.

"Sabrena look at Jim passing."

Ah look up and I see me little brother walking down the corridor. Jim have a head that nobody can't miss and sometimes I does wonder if he head ent too big for he body; ah does wonder how he pass out from inside Mama with that grain ah head. He head big as a base drum.

"Call him for me."

Aliah walked out the door and shouted across the corridor.

"Jim, Sabrena calling you."

Jim turned back and he walked into the classroom; his shirt tucked neatly in his pants and his shoes grinning at me because the whole front open.

He walked close to my desk and he smiled. I smiled back at him.

"Way you going boi?"

"Ah going and play behind the school."

"You eat ah ready?"

"Yes ah done finish eating."

"You want more food?"

Jim whole face light up and I just shove the bowl at him. On a serious note the boy belly big just like his head. He grabbed the bowl and he looked inside it. He looked at me and smiled again.

"Go, go and eat it in you greedy skin; ah doh know if the banana boat does pass in you belly; man for food."

Jim just looked at me and walked out the classroom. I looked at Aliah and we both laughed.

"But Sabrena you know Jim could real eat in truth; how the boy greedy so, he ent say no nah,"

"You could see he and Deon is partner ent?" We laughed again. Deon is Aliah's younger brother and just like Jim they head and they belly big alike.

Chapter 11: My Siblings

I s ah whole set ah characters I have as brothers and sisters; real characters

in truth. I am the fourth of nine children. My sister Dedra is the eldest,

followed by my brother Troy, Elisa, and my two younger siblings, Donelle

and Jim. Princess and Alan lived in Telescope with their father and visited

during the holiday season.

Dedra is about 16. She is red and she feel she is nice but she is not nice at all. Thank God for she little color, because if that wretch was black, shit make with her. She get the colour from Elvyn- she good for nothing father.

Once again, I don't know way me mother find them kinda category of men. Dedra have a sister same age as she self and she ent no twin so you know what that means. Mama does call Elvyn to beat Dedra when she misbehave. They does put her on a grater and tie her on the lamp post behind the house the same way Mr. Errol does tie his cow to graze, and they does beat her mercilessly.

She studying boys and she not going to school when they send her. The girl wasting the money she mother don't even have, but she done tell Mama she don't want school is man she want.

I does just sit down by the back door and look as the whip brace she back; the force at which her father allow the blows to sink, making a loud noise on her skin. Dedra too proud to cry; she think she is rock stone. Mama say is wicked, she wicked. But Mama always have something to say. She is my sister and I love her. She have great potential but is like she ent realising it. I does hear the neighbours talking; they does say bad things about her but I does pretend not to hear and keep it to myself, because if I open my mouth they go make confusion and that's the only time Mama does support she children- is when is time to curse people and disgrace she self.

Me, I don't like that. I find my mother could respect her self better than that, and stop acting like a hooligan. Plus, I does hear the pastor saying that ladies must be seen and not be heard. But it ent look like Mama know about that. They rather be heard than seen.

And Miss Dedra don't like a better sport; she love to jook ants' nest. She is most definitely her mother's daughter. Talk about being a big coward—the girl only have mouth and can't even burst wet toilet paper. She have some evil ways. Sometimes she will cook and not give us food. When she did give us food, she sometimes take all the meat and will only give us gravy.

One Sunday, I ran away with her without telling Mama wey I going. She and Dedra was at war and I wanted to accompany her. We spent the day by one of our cousins in Grand Bras where Dedra complained about the things she was going through at home.

When I came back Mama tell me go for the comb to plait my hair. As I sit down in front her is blows- is like she want to kill me because she beating me non-stop. I can't take all this blows so I leave me jersey in her hand and run. But Mama kinda smart she ent wilding us; she waiting for when we sleeping and wake us up with lash

The next thing is Mama does beat real bad; she ent care what her hand fall on; she letting you have it. It could be a cutlass, iron, ah bat or anything Mama get, she beating you with it.

Later Dedra got married to a man almost twice her age; he works in the prison and they say he have money. But he have a dry weather car. If rain falling nobody can't drive in that old jup jup. I don't like him because he does beat Dedra, very, very bad; her eyes does be black and blue. They say he worked obeah on her because he bring her quite in Trinidad and get married. Each time he beat her, he gets her pregnant. Ah does feel real sorry for her. She cross seems heavy but is like the weight ent affecting her, so she carrying it.

Now there's Troy my big brother. Rumour has it that he can't spell his name. Mama say if he see his name in the road he walking over it and he only going to school for bell and to scrape the pot. Yes he does scrape pot. I does see him doing it on lunch time- he and he partner Brent.

But not one day I see Mama put Troy sit down to teach him anything, but she busy saying bad things about him and calling him dunce. But Troy willing. He does cut the grass around the house, pick up the nutmegs, go under the cocoa and dig yam, and plant things around the yard. He does help the neighbours too and they does give him ah small change. He does give Mama the money to buy things for us to eat.

He like minding animal; he have a goat and he does always take care of it. The goat pregnant and he promised to give me one when it make young ones.

Mama does treat the boy real bad. Sometimes she will cook and not give him food. She does tell him take his clothes and go. He ent have place to go so he does sleep under the house or below the cocoa. His father living in Union but he is ah good for nothing man too. Mama say he never mind Troy and Elisa. She say if he had to give her something for them he wanted her to have sex with him first. He say they not his but that's not true they both have his big nose. Especially Elisa—she nose big like a funnel; it almost covering her face.

Elisa is a real quiet girl—she does more stick to herself; she ent like much friends and she don't talk plenty. She ent lazy as Dedra. Elisa could wash and she could cook. She does a really good job taking care of me and my other siblings. And she have a nice Coca Cola shape and high color. Her hair real long- black and thick. But she ent all that pretty. They say is she nose that spoil her face. Elisa does make fudge and chip chip too. Sometimes she does send me under the cocoa and look for coconut. I does be busy to go and I does peel it and remove the back for her. I not in the grating business tho; ah fraid I cut up me hand so she grates it herself. When she finish, she strain it and put the juice to boil. She does put spice to give the fudge flavour. It gives it flavour in truth.

But Elisa does beat me up; I don't think she like me. It's not her fault. Mama is the cause of that. She does tell them if she see them talking to me what and what she won't do them.

Elisa does move like she kinda dotish too and Dedra does blame the girl for all the wrong thing she do, and poor Elisa agreeing. She saying yes is she and take the punishment. Donelle, Jim, Princess and Alan are my younger siblings. There ain't nothing much to mention about them, except that they hard to deal with.

The house we lived in was an inheritance of my mother from her deceased father, and was shared amongst the ten of us. We were poor, but our clothes were always clean, well except in the mango season, where having a mango fest was evident. We were satisfied-at least we had appeared to be that way. Sometimes things got so bad that we had no food or money for our upkeep and will remain hungry for hours, sometimes even days. It was those days that we would resort to catching a yard fowl, going to catch crayfish in the river, combing below the cocoa to see if we got any fig that was ready, if any coconut had dropped from the tree and in the season where thunder didn't yet roll we will search for yam strings. Once we found the strings, we will then dig deep into the dirt being very careful not to break or jook the yam.Then we gathered everything and made oildown without meat and dumpling.Of course, because we had no money for back and neck or flour.

At times we were lucky to have our neighbours provide food, but we had to keep it a secret from our mother. Since most of the neighbours were considered to be Mama's enemies, she demanded that we stay away from them also. She had this strange belief that we should be enemies with those she labelled as her "enemies" and "rivals". The rest of my siblings obeyed her wishes and sometimes said dirty and unpleasant things to those she was at war with. But it was never my concern. I never liked getting involved in adult matters. And even though there was the fear of being punished, I stuck to my belief.

I respected everyone and always made it my duty to greet those I came into contact with and even offered my assistance where needed. Because of my humility and kind heart, I was loved by many and showered with gifts, prayers and words of encouragement which created a positive outlook in my mind about the future.

But I had a favourite—Mrs. Mary. She was one of the village elderly in her late eighties who moved with the grace of a teenager. She was always pleasant and welcoming- a woman with a big heart, who spoiled me with gifts anytime we came into contact with each other- gifts I had to keep hidden of course, to avoid the wrath of my mother. In my clothes were a candy bar, Cinderella story book and some snacks she had given me not too long ago.

At times on my way from school when no one was around, I will sneak into her yard and assist with whatever she needed to be done. I will fetch water, feed the chickens and gather wood for her fireplace. We would chat a little which is when she told me stories of when she was a little girl. That was a time when demons roamed the streets and it was necessary to be very, very careful. She will even tell me the tales of Anansi the clever spider man, who always had a trick up his sleeve.When she laughed it was a little bit spooky, which sent shivers down my spine. Before departing she will prepare one of her tasty meals. Her meals were the tastiest and were always accompanied by a hot glass of milk.

"Drink doodoo darlin,'" she would say.

"It's good for your brains, one day you will be somebody and raise your mother nose you hear".

I smiled believing in her words that one day I will be successful and end the cycle of poverty.

Before I leave, we would first make sure that the path was clear and no one was in sight. Then I would carefully sneak out and run all the way home, since I was expected to be inside at a certain hour.

Chapter 12: Sex Toy

The months following that first incident went by in a blur. Uncle Jack

continued to use me for his sexual gratification and I continued to suffer

silently. Sometimes when his penis can't go inside me he does rub grease and

when I cry he does tell me shut up. I wish, I could just die and end my

misery. At night I go to bed praying that I don't wake in the morning, but

God not answering my prayers; He ent attending to my supplications. So I have to take what Uncle Jack giving me. Not that I want it but I ent have

nobody to talk to, nor do I have another choice.

School is the usual place, but I can't bring myself to learn anything. I can't stop thinking about what I am going through at home. I'm not too friendly with the other students, because I'm sort of jealous of them. They seem to be enjoying their childhood; they're jovial and happy but me, I'm hurting. I think I'm less than they are. I'm contaminated so I don't want to contaminate them.

I don't have a good relationship with my teachers either. They don't really like me and I couldn't care less, because I don't even like myself either. Mr Ogham is the only one that talks to me - he say I have a good memory because I could remember all the Bible verse he teaches. But he also saying that I ent applying myself, that I can do much better if I pay attention to my work. He ent know what going on so he have a right to assume. Little does he know and I'm not going to convince him otherwise or dismiss his ignorance. Whenever he make them statement I just look at him and smile shyly as if to assure him I was going to take him seriously. Truth is, I don't see myself taking any thing seriously any time soon. He normally would lend me his books, because I love to read. I don't like books with pictures. I rather use my imagination. I always imagine characters as being black. I'm not racist but I don't like how our ancestors were treated. It's difficult to teach me history, or to speak about slavery anytime I'm around. Ah swear ah could vex with you for that.

Some of the teachers call me names; they say I'm dunce as the back of a spoon and my mother should consider sending me to the New Life Organization (NEWLO) to learn a trade. NEWLO is a place for children with hard head who find it difficult to learn academics hence they are placed in NEWLO to see if they will excel. They say me mother must not waste she money and send me in Secondary School.

The kinda thing I does want to tell some of them, but sometimes I does just keep me cool and watch them and shake me head. I don't have the time. But whenever sports is around the corner they try to befriend me, because they need they house to win. I only running because I like to run, its one of the things that make me happy, so their pretensive treatment don't move me, it's what I love.

I had started fighting alot, especially on Fridays. It was like a sport. I would take all what the other children did to me during the week and wait patiently as Friday approached and give them a taste of their own medicine. I does win all my fights. I was not a bully; I was only retaliating to being bullied. I choose to fight on Fridays because the possibility of being punished was unlikely since there was not any school on the following day.

The punishment for fighting was severe strokes accompanied with the punishment of standing up in the burning sun with a chair on your head until the principal decided it was time to put it down. Then it was back to the classroom where everyone made that person a laughing stock and tease them, asking if they was finish cooking from the hot sun, or if they pee clothes had dried. The weak students cried and the strong ones answered back. As for me who was rebellious, there was not a teacher who was going to put me in the hot sun with any chair on my head. No wonder the teachers hated me. It was my attitude, but besides I hated them also.

The bigger children does say I smell ah pee. I does smell ah pee in truth because I develop this don't care attitude, plus lately ah just staying so and wet my pants—ah really don't know what causing that, because that never use to happen before.

Chapter 13: Common Entrance Examinations

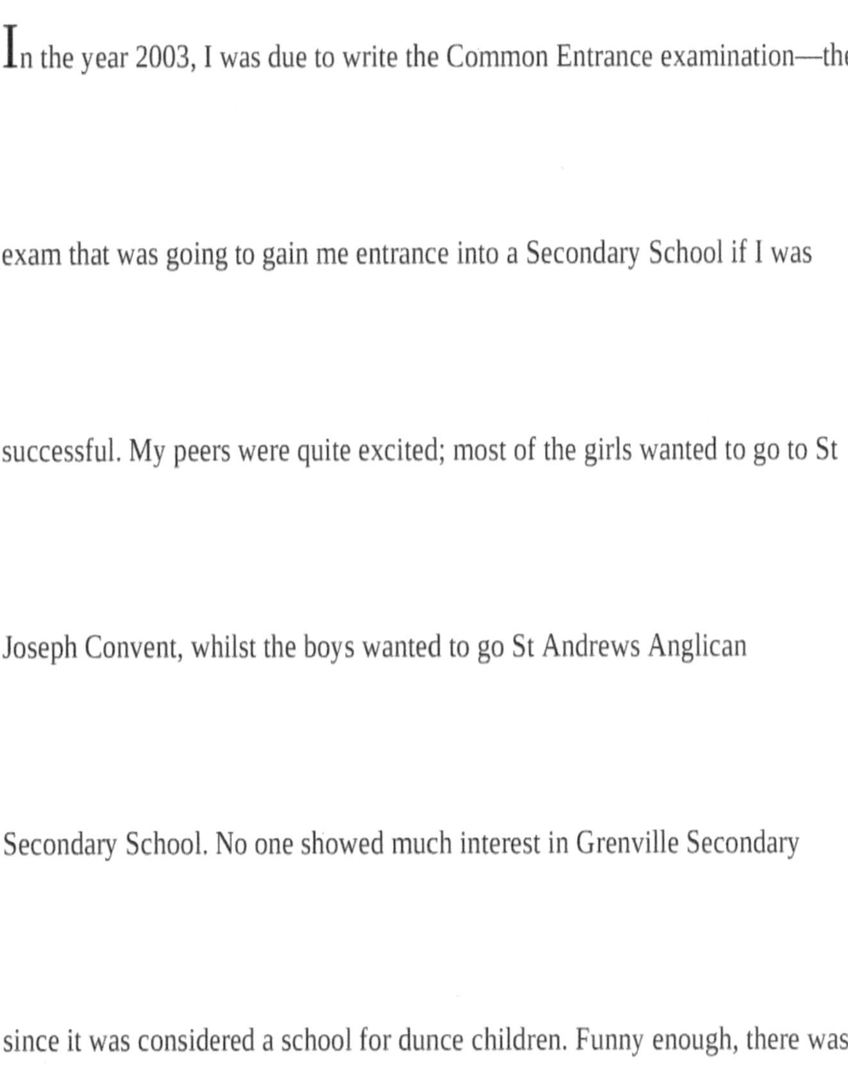

In the year 2003, I was due to write the Common Entrance examination—the

exam that was going to gain me entrance into a Secondary School if I was

successful. My peers were quite excited; most of the girls wanted to go to St

Joseph Convent, whilst the boys wanted to go St Andrews Anglican

Secondary School. No one showed much interest in Grenville Secondary

since it was considered a school for dunce children. Funny enough, there was one of my friends who put his choice of entry as the St Giles Anglican

Primary School. It was rather funny and when we found out we made fun of

him.

As for me I wanted to fail. I was not ready to go into no Secondary School. I did not want to deal with the false pretence of my mother if I was successful. Passing exams was a big thing- it indicated that your child was bright and whenever a child pass, their parents will walk around the village proudly telling everyone and receiving praise. I wanted to fail, so that my mother will be put to shame.

The day of the exam I was late. I was the last to enter the examination hall but the first to leave. The exam was not hard, but I had shaded the wrong answer by spite as a means of failing. As I journeyed back home everyone was asking questions about the exams—all except my mother. I nodded my head in indication that it was good and continued on my way.

The next day of school everybody was saying how the exam was easy, even them dunce children was excited and confident. Aliah was happy too; she say she know for sure she pass and she was getting she first choice. Ah tell her keep she fingers cross and hope for the best. I ent saying much and I ent boasting because I could care less about Common Entrance; I could care less about going in Secondary School.

One month later, results were out and I had secured a seat in the Grenville Secondary School. I was disappointed. I wanted to stay in Munich. I wanted to fail. I wanted people to laugh at Mama and tell her that she child dunce. I wanted her to hold she head in shame. Aliah was not too happy—she pass for

Westerhall Secondary School but she wanted to go St Andrews Anglican Secondary.

Chapter 14: Secondary School

Most of the girls in my class were stuck up and mean— they think they are

Miss Hightitity. Me, I poor. I ent have much so I jamming in me section.

There is this particular group that call themselves the Powerpuff girls—

Bubbles, Blossom and Buttercup. At a time I wanted to fit in so I told them

I'll be called Clip. They laughed and made fun of me so I had decided to stay

far away from them.

I don't have much friends because I'm not popular, but I have a few—
especially Benedict—he is the brother of my cousin Bolo. People does say
Bolo is a good for nothing father because he not minding his child- he always
by a rum shop and every Monday morning he drunk. But that's not any of my

concern—people just don't know how to mind they business.

Bolo is a nice man;he makes me laugh and whenever he stop by from the rum shop and come home, he does kinda ease the tension, taking my mind away from all the bad things I have to go through.

Benedict is a very nice person, although he has two big Bugs Bunny teeth and them girls does call him ugly. He is a Christian boy and he's rather focused. At times we go in the library together but I does get easily carried away, I have too much things on me blasted mind. Oh, and Benedict could cook! He is the best in the Food and Nutrition class—the class that Mrs Grey and long neck Richards teach. Ah can't stand Miss Richards—she have a piggish attitude and she don't know how to talk to people.

So out of the fourty-four children in my class, I'm close with about two. I have other friends but we not in the same Form 1. Some of them in 1S and the others in 1G.

I always in some fight and confusion, and most of the children were afraid of me because I had a really bad temper and I'm not backing down for anybody, not even the teachers, because I ent care about them.

Most of the older children does laugh at me. The reason is because on the day of orientation, I had left my mother because I wanted to pee and I could not see her. So I went in the bathroom without telling her where I was going. Eh heh? The woman din play with me when I get back- talk about bad words and box in me face.

"Ah tired and fed up with you Sabrena. Wey the ass you come out? You think is now I looking for you. Ah tired tell you that you can't disgrace me because I is one woman anyway the donkey kick me ah kicking it back!"

So everyone pointing at me and making fun ah me, they saying I am the girl she mother beat on orientation day. Those that I hear and I ent fraid, I does curse them and tell them hurtful things and they dare not hit me because fight is me middle name.

Once I get suspended for cursing a girl. I told her she was taking man for ah dollar and she was cheap so she had little or no right to talk to me. Besides she was dunce, real dunce- she ent even know how to spell cat. She was fifteen years old and still in Form 1; she was too ashamed of herself. She reported me to the principal and I was suspended without the principal even listening to my side of the story. Me, being afraid of Patsy, I dressed for school every morning. I ent seeing the school house but I going and come back home the exact time I suppose to come home.

I'm really good at Maths and Agriculture Science though, but I prefer Maths especially subsets; something about the circles I find intriguing. The teacher, Mr. Thomas, gave me a certificate for best Math student. When I bring it home for Mama, she ent say nothing. She seems a little proud. She put it in she important bag and that's the end of it.

Much people ent like GSS; they have alot of bad things to say. They say the girls in the school ent good, all they dey good for is to take man and throw children. But we not all that bad. I don't think it's as bad as it sounds. Because the rest ah girl from the other secondary schools bad too- some say dem girls that wearing the cocoa brown more bad than soap seed. But me, i doh like the 'dem say.'

One day they passed a book around the class and they told us to put we house phone numbers just in case our parents need to be contacted. The book reach in front me and I just staring at it. Everybody put they number, but I don't have no number to put because we ent have house phone. But if I don't put a number them children go think I poor. Yes I poor but they go treat me different so I make up a number and put it down. The next day the teacher call me in front the class and embarrass me telling everybody I was a liar and I had no house phone and I had proceeded to put a number. My classmates laughed of course and I was embarrassed.

Chapter 15: Chewing Gum

Some of the children does call me poor and say I is ah church rat and my

family ent have nothing. It's true we ent have nothing but, I doh care; it don't

even bother me anymore.

I walk in class one evening after lunch and when I sit down I feel something cold and sticky on me skirt. I din bother to watch the chair - I just pull it out and sit down, the same way I does pull it out everyday when I come back in the class from lunch. When I get back up, I see my skirt sticking to the chair and everybody looking at me and laughing- even Mary who ent know what today is, watching me and laugh and the two rotten teeth in front she mouth look like it laughing too.I pull my skirt around. When I look is chewing gum. Ah know when I reach home Mama go cut me ass because chewing gum don't come out on you clothes like that - you does have to boil and soak it in hot water.

One piece ah vex take me and I lost all my senses; me temper raise one time. Everybody still laughing.

"Who do that?" I shouted and I'm sure them children upstairs and them in the staff room quite down in the end of the building could hear me.

Nobody ent answer but all the laughing stop. I look and saw Sara bending over to Ruth and whispering something in her ears.

"Somebody best start talking if allu doh want to see ah grey donkey turn blue. If nobody ent say anything, I go damage one of allu eh, and ah dead serious because right now if allu juck me, nun of allu ent getting blood!"

I still making noise and the same time Mr Onswin walked into the class. They say he is we Form Master but I doh like him at all. He always have 'wawet'by he mouth—some big piece ah white thing like the froth that was coming out my grandmother mouth when she catching she stroke.

He can't dress either, and he don't smell nice like Mr Grey —the nice young teacher who does wear some nice clothes and expensive cologne. Ah doh know who tell Mr Onswin bell bottom pants reigning and ah does wonder if he doh have a mirror or a wife home, because no wife in they good head ent making they husband leave they house looking so.

"Sabrena, why you making all that noise? Is quite by the office I stay and hear you. Ah tired tell you that little girls must be seen and not heard. If that's the way you does behave home, don't do it here."

I watch Mr Onswin and I cut up me eye, I watch him up then I watch him down.

"I could make whatever noise I want because me mouth is mines and them stupid idiot in this class put chewing gum on me chair and mess up me skirt!"

He watch me like if he want to say something. He stand up right in front the black board. He take out his eyes on me and face the class with he hand in his pocket and ah serious look on his face.

"Who put chewing gum on Sabrena chair?"

The class was now quiet—nobody ent laughing and giggling and nobody ent leaning over to whisper in anybody ears. Everybody sit up straight and they watching Sir as if he is ah stranger. Nobody ent answering either and you could see on Sir face, that he getting vex.

"So nobody won't answer?" Sir walking around the class now and he tapping everybody desk.

"How about I suspend the whole class?"

I could see the change in everybody facial expression. Nobody ent like suspension because when you get suspended they say it does be hard for you to graduate.

"Sir." I heard the voice and I turned around in the back; It was Massy with her finger up in the air and she hand trembling, "Is Ryan do it," she said,

"Ryan put the chewing gum on Sabrena chair."

I looked at Ryan and all I wanted was just run towards him and grab him by his bat ears. Ryan ears dey like the wings of a plane that ready to take off and when he talk he nose does open like when donkey ready to bray; he perspiration high—high like the cost ah living. Instead of him studying to bathe, he putting chewing gum on me skirt.

Ryan turn around and made the kill sign for Massy. He put he hand by he throat and he pull across he finger. That's a threat and anybody make that threat at me I does fly on them like ah grasshopper and I does beat them real bad.

"Ryan follow me to the staff room."

Everybody know Ryan was going and get some strokes and Sir does beat real hard. As soon as Sir walk out the door the laughing start back. I just changed my chair and take Ryan own, wondering what I go tell Mama when I reach home.

Chapter 16: Narrow Escape

I drop out the bus and walked up Plaisance big hill. No wonder I does run

good in school because is everyday I have to walk up that big hill and

sometime when I ent tired I does run up. But today I walking. I walking and I

thinking about what I go tell Mama about the gum on me skirt.

Ah say good afternoon to Miss Glura when I reached her gap.

"How you doing doodoo?" she asked, smiling at me and the free space in she mouth showing. Miss Glura done lose all she teeth ah ready but she ent care because it does not stop her from eating corn and dumpling. She gum soft, soft like them Sada own and she love to open she mouth. Ah never see more, she just like Mr Eric—he ent have no teeth and always thirsty for talk.

"I dey, I dey," I answered, thinking real hard about the excuse to give me mother because I know is cacolie rod or spice wood ah getting in me backside.

"Ok, ok doodoo study you head in school and make you momma proud you hear?"

"Yes Miss Glura," I replied and sped up the hill.

I smelled the food quite down by Mr Elvin grave—something about

Mama cooking ah does can't miss. She pot does always have a nice smell. I wish she was in a good mood. If only I had money I woulda stop by Mr Brown and buy her a pack ah cigarette—at least it would have calm her nerves and she would forget about the big stain on me skirt.

Ah see Elisa in the pipe as soon as I break the corner. She was leaning over the stand pipe with she big bam bam cock up in the air as if she is ah peacock. She ent see me and I keep walking closer to the gap wey I does plant all them pretty flowers that I water every morning before going to school. I looked at the bitter fence, the rose and the croton in admiration— they growing nice and they reminding me of my childhood—innocent and pretty, just growing, blooming and being happy. Well, until that monster of a man came around and just like the rose, my life was filled with thorns and thistle.

"Elisa girl."

Elisa raised up her head from down in the pocket; her forehead shining and sweat running down she face.

"Aye girl, wah say; you make me fraid you know."

"You too darn coward," I said.

Elisa don't go to school as the rest of us, she never had the chance to do Common Entrance because she was a sickly child, and each time when the exam came around she fell sick and had to be hospitalised. So she does stay at home and help Mama around the house. She does wash our clothes and cook and take care of my younger brothers and sisters. Mama does just make them and Elisa does take care of them. When they cry she walking them and when they mess she wiping they bottom. Elisa is like Mama left hand, but sometimes I does feel sorry for her because when Mama thing take her, she does ask her to go and Elisa does have to sleep under the cocoa too just like Troy because of Mama forbidding her to come in she place.

"You too darn coward for a big girl, I make yuh fraid."

"You better watch you words Miss Lady."

"Sorry, sorry but you too coward in truth."

I walk in the gap and I climbed up the little hill to go down in the yard.

"Good evening Mama." She on the step and smoke coming out from she nose and she mouth and she pulling the cigarette the same way I does pull on the turkey bone to get out the season mara.

"Good evening Miss Oman."

"Mama it have chewing gum on me skirt." The words took it's time to come out ah me mouth and Mama look up and stick she eyes on me; she ent even blinking.

"What you mean it have gum on you skirt?" She take another puff again and I sneezed. I hate the scent of that stinking thing they call cigarettes.

"Some body put it on the chair and I sit down on it."

"Somebody put it down on the chair and you sit down on it?"

"Yes Mama."

"And you expect me to believe that?"

"Yes, well is that Mama."

"So I is ah chupidee now ent? Me is ah papyshow? Because ah never go Secondary School you think you could fool me with cock and bull story?"

Mama laugh, and it sounded like when the breeze blow through dry leaves and scatter the small pieces of brambles. I know it ent no good laugh so I turn on my guards, looking around for my closest escape if I was going to need one.

"Is some man you come out and take and dirty up the back ah you skirt you little whore. Is that I sending you to school to do, to open you stinking dirty legs to take man? That I wasting time and money for?"

Mama's word hit me hard, real hard. It make me heart feel ah kinda a way and my head feel funny too as if it going and burst.

"Which man I come out and take?" Ah wanted to tell her is she man I does take—she big stink, dirty good-for-nothing man. But I stand up shaking me foot trying my best not to answer her. I shake but not with fright but with anger. The kind ah things I does want to tell that woman eh, sometimes I does just have to thank God she is me mother.

"Doh answer me back in me place you kno stinker. If you want to answer anybody go and build you own little joppa, not under mines!"

I watched Mama and wondered for a big woman how she ent have no common sense. Why a woman with no sense had to make all these children—children she can't even hold a normal conversation with because everything for Mama is bad word or to tell people hurtful things.

"I ent answering you; I just tell you what happen. Is Ryan put gum on my chair."

"Listen Sabrena, come out in front of me face before I have the cause to knock you down you hear, and try you best to get that gum off you skirt because my hands ent going on it. If my hands only go on it me name change —I ent Patsy again!"

My foot kicked a stone; I fretted and walked towards the step. I jammed myself in the corner to avoid rushing Mama because I don't want she to push me over and break me neck—not me and that woman.

"Oh ho Sabrena, change you clothes and go in the garden with Jack".

I bite me lips, and up to now I ent answer. Garden again oh boi, poor me under him.

Chapter 17: The Earth's Floor

I walked through the track behind Uncle Jack. He in front and I behind like

a little puppy. He stepped on a branch and it made a loud creepy noise. I

stopped same time because I didn't want to step on the same branch and

something happen to me.

"Darn blasted thing!" He cursed and I steups. In me mind darn blasted thing in truth. Why the piece ah wood never make him fall and break he neck! We pass through the track by the big mango tree and burst out by the river. The river wey we does normally bathe and fetch water when the water in the pipe go.

"Wey we going?" I asked, looking around to see if it have any ripe cashew on the tree so I could ask Uncle Jack to pick it for me. I ent see none and me heart sink.

"We going up in the land by Justin. Just follow me." Ah steups in me mind again all dey. All this blasted walking.

Uncle Jack jumped the river stones and I jumped them too— ah stretching me long legs as far as they could go, because I want to keep up with him. His foot longer than mines and his strides longer too. Ah know if I slack in the back he go punish me. We reach the garden and Uncle Jack put down his bag.

"Come Sabrena, ah want to take you right here."

My heart sank and I felt like if the earth opening up to swallow me; me heart feeling like it dey in me toe and me body get numb, numb. Don't matter how much time Uncle Jack boom me, I can't get use to it. I always feeling worthless and as if my life going to end.

I watched as Uncle Jack spread the fine bag on the ground; he pull it neat, neat and he look around to make sure nobody was watching, but nobody can't really see us wey we dey on top of the hill behind the coconut trees.

"Lay down Sabrena."

I obeyed. I lay down straight on me back and my mind drifting far, far away.

During those times my spirit does really leave me body. It's not that I accustom to it, it's just that I can't do any thing to help it. I listen to the river, the noise it making rushing down the river banks, the stillness of the evening, the little bird singing in the tree and the noise the coconut branch making as it blow in the wind. They were swaying and jamming each other; dancing slowly and the leaves opening up like a fan and closing back with the rhythm of the wind.

His hands glided up my legs, reminding me of his first touch and I held my breath. My heart beating in my chest like an old pan, but I tried to remain calm since it was my tactic of dealing with the pain. In order to not feel much pain I had to keep quiet. The more I co-operate the easier it had become. He tugged at my lower body and I felt the strings of my panty sliding down my legs. I closed my eyes and waited for the dreaded moment to be over. I smelt his scent of vaseline and sulphur (the sulphur Mama had applied to his skin for the rash) and I tried blocking my mind once more. The bird sang again and this time it sounded so sad and lonely, so bitter and cold not merry and happy as it used to. I felt caged in as his body collided with mines slamming his weight against my lower body, easing him self up and slamming himself on me again. I felt my body expanding and pain rush through my skin. I held back the tears, stretching my legs in pain.

"Sweet!" he exclaimed as he ground himself on me, "So blasted sweet".

I ignored his voice and I tried blocking it away too, praying for him to finish and to continue in the pretence game of him being my protector.

Something sting me back and I jerked my body.

"Continue like that Sabrena, ah cuming"

I remained still. The last thing I wanted him to think is that I was participating in his evil, cursing the ants in my mind. Why the hell did it have to bite in my flesh at this time?

He heaved in pleasure and then I felt his weight lift off my body. I counted to sixty and when I opened my eyes he was already covered.

"Put on you clothes and take a rest while I dig the yam for you mother."

I put back on the panty with the big hole in the middle and I remain laying down on the bag with my eyes open wide towards the heavens praying to God for the day all this would end.

Chapter 18: Hurricane Ivan

The principal called an emergency assembly and we all gathered on the land

in the hot sun, just about 12 noon, because we had just come back from our

lunch break. Everybody seemed to be sush sushing.

Mr Ramlogan stood up in front the door. He is really short and he is an Indian. They say he does work obeah because he have alot of little dolls in his office and his office always dark. I don't know much about obeah except that they say is obeah have Caroline thieving and is everything she see she have to pick up.

Caroline hand longer than her foot and once she bring Elisa to thief with her and Police lock them up. Elisa say when the Police came, Caroline had food on the fire and she was cock up watching TV in she bra and tights. Poor Elisa ent even know is break, Caroline break open the people house.

Anyway, Mr Ramlogan have the mic in he hand. He was wearing a blue shirt that have a few little stain and he favourite grey pants—them children say that's his tattoo because he always have it on.

"Teachers and students, we will be dismissing school early today. There is a tropical depression outside and we are warned that it can develop into a hurricane. I want each and every one of you to listen very attentively. Students you are to go straight home. No liming by the fish market; no liming on the bus stand; no branching over to the park. This is serious—go home."

Ah dey wondering to myself what he talking about—tropical depression?

Hurricane? And for once I wished I used to pay attention in Geography class.

"I won't be long here. As soon as I ring the bell I want you all to go straight home."

He finished talking and dismissed the assembly. Everyone was excited because we were going home early. I walked back in the classroom, removed my books from the desk and put them in my bag. I looked around the class and saw Tasha kissing Kelvin- she tongue deep, deep down in he throat and she jaw moving up and down as if she eating Kuma. I looked away pushed in my chair walked out the door and went towards 2G to wait for my friend Rina.

"We going home early girl," Rina said with a big smile on her face, showing all her thirty two teeth. Rina don't like school and I don't like school either. We does wait patiently for the bell to ring - the lunch bell, break bell and the home bell. We does skull classes too and we does go and sit down in the back ah the toilet and talk about people.

"Yeah, but what is ah hurricane?" I asked.

"Girl ah doh really know nah, but is something that does come with plenty, plenty wind and it does blow down people house, and blow out they roof and people does dead."

"People does dead?" I asked in shock. I then realised that a hurricane was a serious thing.

"Yes people does dead. Grandma told me when she was small it had a hurricane—that was plenty, plenty years ago. The name of the hurricane was Janet and it was bad; mostly everybody house mash up, drains block up, trees fall down and alot, alot ah people dead."

"So hurricanes have names?"

"Yes girl." Rina look at me and cross up she eyes as if to ask how you so stupid.

"You ent hear Mr Ramlogan say the name of the thing is Ivan?"

"Oh yes, oh yes he said that. Well we better hurry up and catch the bus."

I grab Rina by her hand and we both walked toward the gate under full speed. I was afraid. I wanted to go home. And looking at Rina's face, I know she was afraid too.

Chapter 19: Ivan The Terrible

I reached home and told me mother about the hurricane. I told her they sent

us home early because there is a hurricane coming. Mama looked at me from

head to toe and laughed. When Mama laughed, she whole face does light up

and she does look pretty, pretty.

"Come Sabrena, you see the sea how it calm?" From our house we could see the sea down in Soubise.

"Yeah it calm Mama, it calm."

"Right, so doh study them; no hurricane ent coming. That's not the first time they sending out warning. Look how much years now they say Grenada getting hurricane and nothing. G for Grenada and G for God. God not going to let no hurricane destroy us."

Mama talking but I listening to the radio (the old radio with the broken handle that does sound as if it have cockroach inside it). Elisa say the radio have a jumbie because one minute it does be working good and the next minute it not working at all.

On the radio, a woman was talking and saying how we should go about being prepared for the hurricane and when it strike. She was calling out some names of schools and churches and asking that people move to them, especially the people living in wooden house because it was more safe. She was saying to buy dry goods too like Crix and tin stuff and to have a search light with batteries.

"Mama you listening what the lady saying?" I taking in everything she saying. Based on how she talking, ah hurricane is ah serious thing and I don't want nothing bad to happen to me.

"Sabrena ah tell you doh worry; stop asking me stupid questions. NaDMA could say what they want—no hurricane ent coming".

"What is NaDMA? '

"NaDMA is some shit. I doh even know—some NGO."

"NGO? But what is NGO?"

"Sabrena when you go in school ask them."

I watched Mama—she big belly pushing out from she jersey and she stand up with she foot bend back. Mostly every body does stand up and bend they foot- well everybody except me. Mama suppose to make baby anytime soon, because she little black bag that look like a suitcase done pack ah ready. Ah hear she telling she husband that the child kicking and like he head move so he go come soon. It's Mama's first pregnancy for him, so like all our other stepfathers, Uncle Jack breed Mama too. He ent care about we living conditions; he doh mind if when the child born it have to sleep on he head. The house done too small for all of us ah ready and in the night we does rush to see who could get the best space on the mattress.

Outside was calm, calm, calm—calm like midnight when everybody sleeping and nothing ent going on - calm like when Mama sleeping and she eyes close and part of she hair hanging down in she face. Mama does sleep and smile and she does look so peaceful and happy. But when she wake that in itself does be a whole different story. Even the dog does have to watch how it bark because she cursing dog and all. Mama does tell the dog all about it whoring mother.

Soon after the weather change completely; rain started to fall and the breeze started blowing. The breeze made a noise like the one Mr Adam does make when he blowing he old dirty flute.

"Like this hurricane thing really serious. Allu come and help me secure some things. Get allu books and put it inside the stove and Elisa start to cook

—it have some corn fish and rice— put ah coconut in it." Mama shouted

Elisa looked at Mama and shake she head in agreement as she walked towards the fireside.

"Use the coalpot girl; doh go outside dey in that weather."

We have a coal pot. Mama say it old like the road because it belonged to she great, great grand father. And we have a coal pit too, just behind the house close to the nutmeg tree, Uncle Jack and Troy does cut wood and make coals. After they pack the wood they does throw some grass and then cover it with mud and leave it overnight. The coals does come out real nice and pretty. But they does have to use plenty, plenty water to out it.

We does sell most of it, but we does keep back some, Mama does more use it to iron we school clothes. We doh have fancy iron that working with current like Rosalie and them. We have a heavy metal iron and when it hot Mama does use a cloth and wipe it, then press we uniform neat, neat, neat!"

I grabbed my books while Donelle and Jim grab theirs too and we threw them in the stove. It's an old stove Mama's sister give her. I ent know why she never just throw the stove outside for the rubbish truck to pick it up, because not one burner in the stove working and Mama just have it in the corner pack up in the kitchen taking up space we done doh even have.

Rain falling heavier now and it sounding like when we throw gravel on the roof- it hitting the galvanise hard, hard. The wind continue to howl.

"The tropical storm Ivan is quickly developing into a hurricane; citizens are asked to take outmost caution and be prepared. Remember to evacuate if your houses are not safe enough," the radio announcer said.

The lady on the radio talking and she repeated the safe houses again. Persons in my area were advised to go to the Holy Innocent Anglican School, the Catholic Church in De Blandeau or the Community Centre in Union.

Elisa in the veranda blowing the fire to catch and I sit down looking at her. She have one hand on the coal pot and the other on the ground. She eased herself up a little and blow the fire. The fire catch and she dusted off her hand.

"Allu, allu get ready we going by Wake Up." Mama shouted above the heavy wind.

"This hurricane business really serious; ah doh trust this old house."

The weather had taken a turn for the worst; the rain had eased up, but the wind was blowing heavy in all directions. We grab all that we had to and run towards Wake Up house. The pot was still on the fire so we had to run with that too.

"Elisa we go finish coooking in Wake Up veranda," Mama shouted again.

As if waiting for us to settle, the wind started blowing heavier. We wrestled up the hill like Curlan's old bus, while the wind was singing with a rage, shaking the trees. I looked outside as the mango tree bow and piece of her branch flew away straight under the cocoa.

It was just about 6 p.m. and the eye of the hurricane was indeed over Grenada. Mama started taking things serious when the pot that was on the coal pot fly straight out the veranda.

"Allu come, come lets pray!" I hear Mama say.

Pray? I asked myself. *Pray*? Never in my life Mama had asked us to pray so I was a little bit surprised. I wanted to laugh but I know if I did I was going to be punished, so I just look at Donelle and she look at me. Donelle is about nine but she very intelligent. She does always place in the first two in her class.

"Let's read the Bible too, ah doh want to dead," Elisa chip in.

No I was not going to hold the laughter anymore.

"But Elisa ouii, since when you want to read Bible eh, allu hear bout hurricane so allu turn Christian?"

Mama watch me one bad eye. If I cudda take back me words ah wudda take it back.

So we prayed and read the Bible. We read Psalm 23:The Lord is my Shepherd. But we praying and reading ent change anything because the wind blowing heavier. We all inside now but we peeping through the window. The wind making real, real noise and we could hear things falling.

"Oh gawd allu the roof gone!" Mama shouted with panic in her voice. "Look at it flying and Miss Brenda roof gone too. Look it have a roof in the road."

Galvanize was flying like the little jet we normally made in class from paper and fling across the classroom. But nothing ent happening to Wake Up house. Only thing is the dust and the funny smell. It's Wake Up and she brother living there, but they head ent normal. Wake Up brother does walk the road and talk to he self and people say he does not bathe and he don't change his clothes either. From the time I know Mr Zack is one clothes he have on.

We made our beds in Wake Up room. I'm laying down in the end and Uncle Jack in the middle of me and Mama. The wind continue to make its commotion outside. There's nothing anybody could do so we tried to sleep. I feel Uncle Jack hand sliding up my legs. I push them away and drag myself up a little.

"Come up Sabrena, doh lie down on the bare flooring."

I remained where I was, conscious of the fact that he was trying to have sex with me, right besides my mother, not even being mindful that his pregnant wife was lying there. I did not budge!

"Patsy, tell Sabrena come out of the cold floor." I was hesitant.

"So Sabrena you can't blasted hear?" Mama shouted. "Come up on the blasted sheet, come closer to Jack."

Uncle Jack pull me and his hands slide into my panties.

Whenever he tried abusing me, my soul normally felt like it was leaving my body, I was always tense and frightened. Uncle Jack hand inside me now, making circular movement with his fingers again. I opened my mouth to shout, and he pinched me hard in my back. I wrenched and screamed in pain.

"Stop you blasted noise, before I put you outside in the hurricane. So because Jack tell you come closer you bawling?" Mama shouted.

I shake my head at Mama words as I felt Uncle Jack penis inside me. He had entered me from a backward position. The pain was unbearable but I knew, I had to take it and keep quiet.

The destruction from Ivan was indeed great and it was reported that a few people had lost their lives. Everything had changed. Nothing about the Plasiance I knew all my life was the same. Most of the trees had fallen and the road was covered with mud, roof tops, clothing, galvanise and even dead animals. It was so flat that we had a clear view of De Blandeau and even Union. We were warned to remain indoors until we were advised differently.

Mama was having pain and the baby was coming. I can't remember much except that Mama left for the hospital. How she reach I don't know because all the roads blocked and no vehicles were running because there was no place to pass.

All I know is four days later Mama return with a baby boy and people telling Mama to call him Ivan and they say he go grow to be a strong boy because he born during the hurricane. But she say Ivan was too terrible and she not calling she son so.

Uncle Jack boom me all the days Mama gone. It's like he sat down and prayed for night fall to abuse me.

Mama now make baby so she good for a few days, but things not the same. We have to wash in the river now and we using the coal pot more regular- is ah good thing we had coals. The hurricane really changed alot ah thing. All who use to play they too good to go in the river, washing in the river now and they drinking the river water too. Mama say it should choke them because they too blasted hypocrite. She say they does play too high and mighty.

Sometimes Mama does pass she remarks for them people to hear too. She does wait until they passing and say "Jucko to ah you, they washing in the river too," and Mama mouth loud—it like a base drum. They does pretend not to hear Mama and walk fast, fast. Sometimes I does wonder if she ent fraid somebody hold her and beat her, but Mama could fight too.

Chapter 20: Sorrow

I always wanted to speak out, but besides having no one to speak to I knew

how society was going to perceive me. I prayed for strength—strength to

stand up; strength to be bold and strength to seek help. It was becoming

overwhelming and I grew tired of his abuse; of him having me whenever he

wanted and using me as his sex toy—me his own stepdaughter. Whilst he

pretended for others that he was my protector and that he adored me, my days were spent worrying and my nights were spent in tears. I knew no peace and

deep within me, all I felt was sadness. Besides, I knew what he was doing to

me was wrong and I could not continue with his abuse. I wanted it to stop and

above all I wanted justice.

There were days when I was overcome with suicidal thoughts and depression; it was impossible to keep those thoughts from coming. They were overpowering me, leading me to believe that the only solution to my misery was death. My first attempt was the drinking of Sevens poison, but to my greatest disappointment, nothing much happened except vomiting.

My heart grieved within me. What I felt was more than emptiness. There was absolutely no peace. I wanted freedom, breakthrough and most of all I wanted to be rid of the situation. There was no way I could stop reiterating the need for that monster of a stepfather of mines to stop having sex with me. And above all I wanted someone to confide in, someone to talk to about my situation, someone to assure me that everything was going to be all right.

I felt less than the person I was, feeling rejected, lost, betrayed, having no support system, no one to talk to, not even my mother.

I became rebellious, not only at home but with my teachers. I was always distant around my peers since I thought they were better than me. My performance in school was terrible and I struggled for the last position. I was in shambles; highly disoriented, dysfunctional and broken. There were times I tried sending clues to my mother, but they were ignored.

My mother constantly accused me of sleeping around with guys; she referred to me as a whore, prostitute, 'drag-a-bat', good-for-nothing, clothes pin, amongst other names. Her accusations were not true since I was not sleeping around with any one. The only sleeping around that was taking place was with me and that stinking creature she referred to as her husband.

It was during the time of those accusations I will say, "What u have to know, you ent know it." I could not remain standing or in close proximity to her after saying that, of course. My mother was quite a violent and abusive person. She would make some silly remarks, after which she would venture to throw my clothes outside, asking me to come out of her place and go and live with my men and them.

She claimed I was not her responsibility and if I continued living under her roof, one day she will poison me,since it was cheaper and easier for her to bury me, than to take care of me and constantly see me around her.

She even went as far as burning my bookbags, school shirt, socks and other learning materials she had purchased with her money. Travel arrangements was made with Mr Brown, a bus driver in the area, where he was paid monthly for taking me to and from school. There were days when she went as far as telling Mr Brown don't take me on his bus, and if he wanted to take me she was not going to pay. He did not take me of course and those days I was forced to stay away from school.

Sometimes when I was fully dressed for school, she will tear down my shirt and take away my tie. Without a school tie I could not pass the security. There was no excuse for not wearing a tie, none whatsoever, and our school rules were quite strict. Failure for wearing a ribbon normally resulted in suspension.

I was in Form Two at the time and the abuse was still continuing and no one, not even my mother, teachers or counsellors could have guessed my predicament. My absenteeism, disrespect, don't care attitude, lack of proper hygiene, drop in academic performance and loudness were never one day questioned by anyone. Instead I was labelled as a disrespectful child and constantly reminded that I will reach nowhere in life.

Chapter 21: Alone

I was affected emotionally, physically, socially, psychologically as well as

spiritually. It was hard for me to trust people and I had started withdrawing

myself. There were times when I tried to avoid my stepfather, because I knew

whenever he got the chance to be alone with me he was going to abuse me.

There was not a place he did not sexually violate me—in the river, under the cocoa, in the house, beneath the house. He had no control of his fantasy, no conscience to even notice what he was doing was wrong. He pretended not to realise that I was hurting, that what he was doing to me was devastating me and tearing me apart.

I was always punished whenever I tried avoiding him. He would complain to my mother that I was getting out of control, I was beginning to have my own way, I was smelling myself and how I was growing to like the street. She drank whatever soup he feed her and she would beat me mercilessly. At times he joined in and punished me also. I sometimes wondered if my mother was a witch or if she was under his spell. How could she be so blind and supportive of his evil?

Yes, he was the breadwinner of the house, he was the one that worked and provided, but how the heck did that give him the right to do what he was doing. Besides, my mother was not a cripple; at times I wondered why she did not get up and fend for herself instead of depending on that filthy bastard. I sometimes wonder if the vulnerable position my mother put herself in would end.

I prayed believing that one day the good Lord whom we serve, was going to open her eyes to reality—open her eyes to see what was going on around her; open her eyes to pay more attention to her responsibilities; open her eyes to see that her beloved husband was not a contributing factor, but rather a predator to her family. But my mother was a careless being; it was clear that he had her tied around his finger.

I had two best friends when I was in Munich school—Aliah and Neren. We were friends from since childhood. Sometimes I wished I was still that innocent child. We did lots of crazy things together. Neren however, had migrated to live with her mother in New York, so that left me with Aliah as my only best friend.

Before my abuse, I had other friends that I had once enjoyed doing things with. We played together, went on hikes, shared lunch, sat down and told stories, amongst other fun activities. We sometimes cursed and said mean things to each other, but before long we were all friends again. Oh how I missed those days!

Aliah and I had a rather close relationship. We were so close that oftentimes I would sleep over at her place, share her meals, bed and even clothing. We had alot in common. We were both athletes and had succeeded in cheating to be in the same house. We were always winning because we were both star athletes. But now we are in two different secondary schools. We are still close but not as we used to be, which made dealing with my pains even worse.

I was still praying for God to give me the strength to seek help. Secondary school did not change anything; staying away from my stepfather did not change anything either; in fact it made matters worse.

Chapter 22: Reporting The Abuse

I had reached a point, where enough was indeed enough. At last I had

mustered the courage and strength to speak out and stand up for myself.

Things at home were not getting better; in fact they were getting worse. It

was so bad that I was beginning to hate my mother. I was constantly punished

and embarrassed for no particular reason. She used every given opportunity

to remind me of the hatred she felt towards me.

I was tired, tired of being abused, tired of being made to feel guilty, tired of crying, tired of thinking it was my fault and tired of blaming myself. Why was I being made to feel guilty for a crime I did not commit?

It was a morning of school and I decided to visit Social Services. I had made some indirect inquires and had found out the location. No one was concerned as to the reason I was asking for the location and I was happy since it not only saved me from explaining but it also saved me from having to think of a lie.

As I made my way towards the building I was overwhelmed with fear and emotions. But a greater part of me wanted to get rid of the monster that was tearing me apart, so I was determined to speak to someone.

This secret I was forced to keep was affecting my everyday life and my entire being. Crying was the order of my day. Whenever I was alone I cried bitterly. I even took breaks from class and went to the bathroom, shut the door and cried. I knew crying was never going to help but it made me feel better.

I had also resorted to cutting myself. I always had a spare razor blade that I used to cut my wrist. As I cut, I would ignore the pain and watch in satisfaction as the blood flowed from my body. The people who saw the cuts on my hands referred to me as "follow fashion", saying I wanted to be like the white girls on television and that I was dottish. I did not blame them of course because they had no idea of the bullshit I had to face or the pain I was going through.

I was really, really tired of my wicked, good for nothing, egocentric devil, using me for his sexual gratification. He used me when he felt like it, how he felt like and as much as he wanted to. The bastard even made me perform oral sex, to which I always had the urge to bite off his penis. With tears in my eyes I performed this evil act as he groaned and enjoyed himself. It was his groans that always annoyed me. What the hell was he enjoying? It always boiled my stomach and made me very, very, angry.

As I got closer to the building, all sorts of questions and concerns were running through my mind. What if they never believe me? What if I was blamed? What if I was asked to bring my mother? I was only thirteen. Were they going to allow me to make the report on my own? Were they going to victimize me? There was only one way to find out and I prayed that they would take me serious. If not, I was going to kill myself. I had made up my mind to end my life and all the misery.

I walked into the building dressed in my school uniform. As I entered the door, I was greeted by the receptionist. She was warm and it made me relax a little bit. Her smile did not just light up the room; it gave me hope and motivation that everything was going to be alright. I walked towards her and was asked my purpose of visit. I told her I wanted to speak to a Social Worker. I was then asked to provide my name and address. She gave me a book where I entered the details and then I was asked to have a seat.

I made myself comfortable on the chair as I gazed around the room. The office space was beautiful—there were flowers in the corner, a television set and some magazines. There was also a water dispenser and even though I was thirsty I remained seated because I had no idea how it worked and I was too ashamed to ask.

The receptionist was on the phone talking to someone, letting them know that there was a young lady outside wishing to speak to a Social Worker. Three minutes later someone emerged; it was someone I knew—Mr Charles. I knew him because he was once in charge of the Sapodilla Home which was located in my community. He looked at me and I looked back at him and we both smiled.

"What are u doing here Sabrena?" he asked. There was still a smile on his face.

"I'm here to talk to someone," I said shyly.

"Follow me," he said.

I followed him as he walked through the door. There were many other offices each of which had a different sign. His office was on the left hand side of the building and as I followed him in I gazed around. I gazed at his desk, the portrait on his wall, the picture of his family and his computer which was covered with dust. He was now digging through his papers with a pen in hand and looking at me. I felt a bit uneasy and I prayed that he kept digging so at least the time I had to speak will be delayed. There was silence and it was broken by him.

"So why are you not in school?" he asked. He did not wait for a reply but continued, "You've being behaving bad Sabrena; your mother was here complaining quite recently. She said you started having boyfriends and that she can't talk to you."

"Boyfriends? Me?" I asked quite shocked.Mama was actually here.

"This isn't true Sir." I made it clear to him that I am away from school because I want to make a report.

"A report?" He was looking at me with a puzzled look on his face - a look that was more than mere curiosity.

"Yes a report."

"But you can't make a report without a guardian."

"I have no guardian Sir, no guardian whatsoever and I need to make this report. I'm tired. I cannot continue with all this."

He looked at me with a puzzled look on his face, adjusted his seat, shook his head and tapped his hands on his desk.I was certain of one thing; I was not going anywhere until he listened to what I had to say. He will have to listen to me, because I have no guardian here to stand with me.

"So what's the report?" he asked.

"I-I-I." I was stammering. This is something I never actually did before.

"I'm sexually abused," I said.

He sat up from his chair with hishand resting on his desk.

"You what?" he asked. I wondered if he did not hear me, or was he playing dumb or stupid.

"I'm being sexually abused." I repeated.

"You need to understand that such an accusation is serious Sabrena".

"I am serious Sir."

I was biting my nails and staring at the flooring that was a bit stained.He was still looking at me, not saying a word but staring in my direction. It was as if he was trying to make sense of all I just said.

"I'll take a report then," he said, "But know that we won't be putting you back in that house if what you are saying is true."

He pulled out a paper from his desk and asked that I relate my story.

Mr Charles took notes while I told him everything -from the time the abuse started, the threats my stepfather made to me, the attitude of my mother, the nights I had to sleep outside, her refusal to give me food, how she prevented me from going to school, the nature of her physical abuse and the names she called me. I told him how much I wanted a breakthrough, my desire for the abuse to stop and my lack of academic performance. I told him everything and he recorded every detail.

He then asked for my mother's number, which I was sort of reluctant to give, but I obeyed and gave it to him. He also informed me that he needed to involve the police since it was a police matter and I needed to be examined before anything else was done. He asked me to leave the room since he wanted to phone my mother in my absence.

When I joined him five minutes later, he told me that my mother doubted my story; she said it was not true. I felt hurt once more. For heavens sake what was wrong with this woman! Why did she say to the Social Worker that I was lying?

"Don't worry," he said. "The examination will prove everything."

He accompanied me to the police station where I gave an official report and once again I had to repeat the heart wrenching story. I was a bit more comfortable because it was a female office and she was rather compassionate. It was someone I knew also; she was one of my classmates' mother

After relating the story, my eyes were filled with tears. She hugged me, rocking me gently, and assured me that everything was going to be alright, and I had nothing to be afraid of. But I was afraid - afraid of what others was going to think of me, afraid of how my mother was going to react and afraid of my stepfather. What if I was not protected? What if he stayed true to his threats and killed me?

"We need to take you to be examined, and we need to arrest that good for nothing stepfather of yours," she said.

Chapter 23: The Examination

They took me to the General Hospital in St George's. The hospital is huge

and beautiful. One can stay on top of the hill and look down into town. From

there you can also see those cruise ships docked in the harbour. In the night

the ships light up like a Christmas tree. The Cruise ships bring tourists who

buy all kinds of spice. They always wear straw hats and some of them have

pink skin.

Just over the hospital is a fort. The last time I came to this hospital, Mama said Bishop was killed at that fort. I don't know much about Bishop because I was not yet born.

They brought me in a room. The female office and a doctor accompanied me. I was asked to undress. Ah don't like people to see me naked so I was scared and ashamed. I have plenty pwel and I don't want them to see it. The room had a small bed that could be adjusted. I watched as the doctor walked towards a cupboard, open the door, pull out some gloves and put them on her hands. My heart was beating really fast and I was feeling so ashamed.

"Take out you clothes and lie down darling," the doctor said to me.

The police woman on seeing my discomfort bent down and said to me,

"It's okay to take off your clothes; no one is going to hurt you and the examination is very, very important for the arrest."

So I removed the skirt and ah take out me panty.

"Climb on the bed dear and do as I say."

I opened my legs and she inserted her finger. Opening my legs reminded me of all the times I had to open them for my stepfather. It was traumatizing but I had to do what I had to do. The doctor was speaking to the police and telling her that my hymen was broken and that I was not a virgin.

"Put back on your clothes darling. You see it was not that hard."

I dressed myself and I kept my head down because the doctor and the police knew what below me looked like and it was difficult for me to face them. The police woman was real angry; I was seeing it on her face. When we went back to the van she said to the next officer, "We going for him as soon as we have enough evidence."

Chapter 24: Arrested

In the report, I provided two addresses—the one where my stepfather was

working and the other one where we reside. My stepfather was a farmer; he

used to work for Brother Jackson, planting things and picking up his

nutmegs; he used to cut the grass and sometimes he had to go with Brother

Jackson and sell the produce. Uncle Jack does work real hard, but he just

wicked and he does pretend to be the best father. He pretends that he loves and care for me so much. He does say I ent taking me time and bathe and

Mama does make him bathe me. When he washing my vagina he does finger

me; it doesn't hurt so much as the first time because I have grown

accustomed to it now. If I say ah go bathe me self, Mama would start cursing.

He is good at manipulating; he is a very worthless man. If Uncle Jack got a

chance he changing me pad and all.

I was asked to remain seated on the bench in the police station. They told me that they were going to pick up me stepfather. I was not crying but I was sad with all kinda things running through me mind. I sat close to the window peeping outside. The street was real busy. It was just after lunch and everybody seemed to be going about their business.

Next to the police station is a bank and also a bus terminal and not far away is the fish market—the place where people always making noise.

"Aye nice lady buy some jacks." A man said.

"Boy go with you stale fish; you feel ah want me tongue scratch me."

He looked at her and stretched his mouth, "Is money you don't have that's why you behaving so."

She ent study him. She continued walking. Ah want to laugh but I too sad. I does wonder how the police does work with all this noise; but it's like it don't bother them because they accustom. Behind the police station is a port where the boats that going to Trinidad docks.

About an hour later they returned with my stepfather. He was wearing ah brown pants, dirty with stains; his water boots on his feet and his black working jersey. They put handcuffs on his hands and was escorted by a male officer. He ent look scared. He walked in not looking around, but he saw me and he watch me in a kind ah way that made me feel uncomfortable.

"No eye contact with the victim!" the policeman shouted.

"Bravo, give me the key for the cell."

They were going to put Uncle Jack in the dark place—the same place they put Troy the other day for breaking open the people shop. Troy say inside dey real dark and the concrete cold—that's wey you have to sleep until you get bail or they send you down Richmond Hill. Troy never went Richmond Hill; he just spend forty-eight hours in the cell.

Ten good minutes ent gone yet and Mama reach in front the police station ah ready. I was hearing she voice. Mama was bawling. I looked outside and she have she hand on her head and tears running down she face. She wearing she white jersey and she floral skirt she sister send from Trinidad.

"Oh God, oh God me husband!" Ah hear Mama saying. "Me husband innocent; let go me husband. Allu can't lock up me husband!"

People start to gather and they looking around. One thing with Grenadian people is that we real fass; we like to mind people business, but Mama ent really business, she making she noise.

Mama walk closer to the station and spot me; well is now self the thing start.

"You—this dirty little whore they call Sabrena, you go and take you man and dem and you telling people me husband rape you? You little drag-a-bat, sketel, Jezebel, drain jucker, mother harlot. You little good-for-nothing. It will never ever be well with you. Ah man must kill you; they must find your body in a drain somewhere. Man go take you from the four corners of the earth. Your life will be miserable. You won't amount to anything good in this life. I tell you that!"

You would swear is a stranger Mama talking to. What kind of mother says these wicked things to her child? What kind of mother does disgrace she self like that in public? I felt hurt, real hurt. Mama's words were piercing through my heart. If she was not me mother I swear I was going outside and pick up a big stone and burst she freaking head. Who the hell she was calling a whore and prostitute? Darn dunce and stupid woman—and Mama ent finish yet. Mama sit down on the ground and dragging she bottom.

"Tu manuel, tu manuel, curse have to follow you!"

Ah wish a piece ah bottle could sink deep down in she backside. She throwing she curse and I praying silently for God to send them bad wishes back to the pit of hell.

The police walked out and tell her she making too much noise and she have to leave. She say she not leaving without she husband and if they want her to move they must come and move her.

"Oh god, oh god how I go mind them children? How I feeding Azim and dem? Jack is the only one that does provide, but if you head was not freaking hard, you wudda never end up in this situation. Ah did warn you with that black ugly girl they call Sabrena. Ah did tell you stay away from her, now look she make police pick you up. Oh gawd, what ah go do?"

Mama took some deep breaths before she started back again, roaring up as a vehicle changing gears,

"And you, this Sabrena, ah doh want to see you with me eyes; just know I is not you blasted mother. Don't tell people you is me child, in sickness, death or fire. Doh come around me. Ah serious eh. You know because if you come around me you go sorry. Ah matter of fact, take out all the school clothes you have on you and give me; is me husband money wey spend for it. Ah sure the panty under you is he money spend for it too!"

Chapter 25: Mangroves

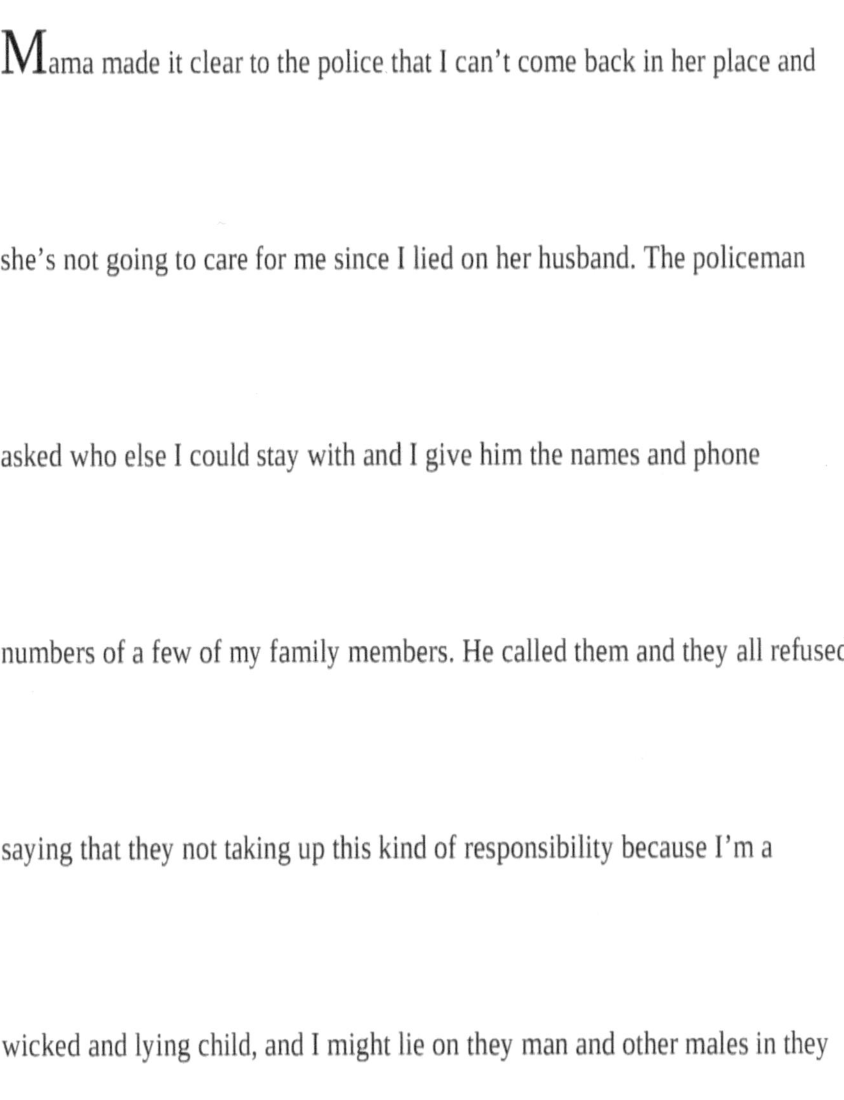

Mama made it clear to the police that I can't come back in her place and

she's not going to care for me since I lied on her husband. The policeman

asked who else I could stay with and I give him the names and phone

numbers of a few of my family members. He called them and they all refused

saying that they not taking up this kind of responsibility because I'm a

wicked and lying child, and I might lie on they man and other males in they household to get them in trouble.

After trying with no success, the policeman asked me to follow him to the van because he had to drop me back to Social Services to see if they could find a place for me.

They had given me some food—rice and dry peas with stew chicken and vegetables, but I had no appetite to eat so I just placed it on the bench besides me. I ent eat but my belly full.

Ah followed the policeman to the vehicle. People were looking at me and whispering; some was even pointing fingers.

"That's the wicked little girl. Children these days real bad and wicked," someone remarked.

I was too embarrassed to look back.

The police vehicle was clean and the driver put on the AC, but ah doh too fancy the idea of driving up and down in the police vehicle; it making me feel like a criminal. It was a short drive—just to make the block and we reach back to Social Services. We coulda walk but them police too lazy, but I glad for the little ride. Mama once told us the only time them police does move fast is when they hear about drugs. She say they does only pretend to burn it, but they does keep it for dey self and eat ah food.

The vehicle pulled up in the car park and I opened the door and stepped out. The policeman opened his door and stepped out too. Using his hands he ushered me inside the building. Mr Charles was still there and the policeman was explaining that I had nowhere to stay.

"Well, we doh have nowhere to put her," Mr Charles was saying.

"What about family members?"

"Nobody ent want her, so you will have to do something."

Mr Charles scratched his bald head and shifted the weight off his foot. Is like he wondering what next to do.

"As you know the Sapodilla Home closed down and we don't have much facilities for children. There is the emergency shelter but them ent have space."

"You have to do something," the policeman said, "We can't leave the child on the street; besides she is ah little girl."

I was feeling really bad. Nobody ent want me. I kinda regretting I make the report because it look like I end up in deeper waters.

"We go find someway. The only place I can think of now is Mangroves, but Mangroves is not a home for children; it might not be the best environment for her."

"Put her dey, until you find someway else," the policeman said as he shook Mr Charles' hand and walked out the door — his black shining shoes making 'coks-e-coks' sounds.

Mr Charles was still scratching he head and he looking at me as if he had seen a ghost. He was wearing a purple shirt tucked in his black pants. He had on black shoes but it ent shining like the policeman own. I coulda see me face in the policeman shoes because it shining so much.

Mr Charles told me I should have a seat that he going and organise to drop me in Mangroves.

"Wey Mangroves is?" I asked.

"Sauteurs," he said and disappeared.

I knew where Sauteurs was—it was the historic Parish; the place wey they say the Caribs had jumped off. If you see how tall the cliff is ah doh know how them Carib jump over that. I does pass through Sauteurs when I going Gouyave to visit my brother Devon. It's a long ride and ah does enjoy it. I does make sure I get a seat by the window so I could see how the water in St Mark does splash up on the wall, reaching all in the road and making the whole place wet. I like Gouyave. It's a nice place and the people don't sleep. So I have a little idea where Mangroves is but Sauteurs is ah big place so I don't know where exactly.

When he returned, he told me a vehicle was going to come to pick me up and that Mangroves was going to be my new home for now and that I was to be on my best behaviour and follow the rules. I shook my head in agreement but deep down I was frightened because I had no idea what to expect. He said the people in the home were expecting me and that he was going to pay a visit soon. He gave me his number and I wrote it down in my diary. He said I should call him if I had any concerns.

The driver that came to drop me in Mangroves was short and black. He favour a dwarf and he ent too good looking either; he nose big and he lips thick; he have a big moustache and he head shave clean. Ah dey looking at him and wondering if he have a mirror. Is either he ent have a mirror or he not in he right head, because he ent looking right. But he friendly, which is ah very good thing. I don't think he have another choice because he can't have all the bad traits.

He was driving them little white bus with seven seats- the one that Brother James have, but his more newer and it cleaner too.

"Small girl you ok?" he asked me.

I looked up and nod at him, because I not in the mood to talk; I thinking about alot of things. I thinking about all the bad things Mama say to me and wondering if it will actually happen. They say curse does follow children and I don't want Mama's curse to fall on me.

I slept the whole way. When the driver woke me up I saw a big white building. It was already night and the crickets were making their usual noise. We were parked in front of a gate and a lady was walking toward us; she was wearing her security uniform - black jersey and black pants. He went out the vehicle and walk towards the gate but I was not hearing what he saying to the woman. I put me hand on me chin and looking at the surroundings. Close to wey we were parked was a red bus and a small board house. I did not see any other house; all I seeing is bush and fig trees. He returned to the car and the lady opened the gate and told me come in. I said goodnight and she answered with a smile.

"Whats your name sweetheart?" she asked with a smile on her face.

"Michelle" I replied. I was not going to be called Sabrena anymore.

"So why you here?" she asked. Her question made me feel uncomfortable. How I going to tell her that I was abused and that my mother refused to care for me?

Before I could answer I saw the big door open and a short well-dressed woman walking down the stairs. She walked towards me and took my bag. She smelled really nice and her face looked nice too.

"Welcome. We are happy to have you," she said.

I looked her up and down before I said anything.

"My name is Miss Mitchell and I'm the manager. Dinner is ready so come in," she said.

I walked up the stairs behind her. The place has a real nice view of what I guess is Sauteurs town; plenty of lights and it looks rather beautiful. She opened the door and we entered a big hall. In the far corner was a big table. Then I saw a girl run across the room.

"That's Denna. Denna ent too right in she head."

Denna grinned and danced at me. She missing she two front teeth and ent have no hair on she head either.

"Miss Mitchell, Miss Mitchell I want some more food," she said.

Denna's feet were white too and she was scratching her skin; she moving like she was slow. She was staring at me without saying ah word as she bit into her jersey. Denna seemed to be a big girl about twenty-five so I wondering why she behaving as if she is ah little child.

"Go in your room Denna and get some rest. You eat ah ready?"

Denna skipped pass me and ran in the opposite direction; she pulled the blue curtain then disappeared.

Ms Mitchell introduced me to the other staff; she told them I was the new resident. I pulled up me skirt just to find something to do and I nodded at them. The cook seems like a nice woman and I could smell the scent of tuna; maybe that's what they had for dinner.

Ms Mitchell asked if I was hungry. I lied and told her I ate already. She then asked the caretaker to take me to my room.

The room was big and it have three big beds. That's something I not accustom to because at home we does sleep on the mattress and when we get up we does have plenty, plenty sponge in we hair. But this bed different; it big and it pretty and it's covered with a pretty, pretty sheet. It have a ceiling fan too. Miss James turned on the fan and the cold breeze hit me face and goose bumps come up all over me body. It have cupboards too she tell me to put my clothes there. We ent have cupboards home but my aunty have so I know what it is. We accustom putting our clothes in barrel and searching through it when we want something to wear. She showed me the bathroom and told me I could go ahead and bathe when I am ready. She then left shutting the door behind her.

Chapter 26: Reminiscing

I sat down on the wall just in front the cashew tree and plenty things

running through my mind. The breeze blow and piece of hair fly in me face.

It tickled me and I laughed to myself.

I don't like being in the house; it's too noisy since Debby always shouting at somebody or shouting for something.

Debby is one of the residents; she's an albino. Her skin white, white and her hair white too. I don't like albino people, because Mama say they not normal. Dey say Debby can't see but I don't believe that because Debby always in somebody business.

Debby have a little son too, but he's a special child. He "stupidee", that's how they does call people like Debby son. He always walking around and dribbling on he self and everybody, even the workers, does scorn him. He makes some funny noise too that make him sound as Miss Mavis' old dog. Some of the residents and workers does wring his ears when nobody ent watching and he does run in the room and try to complain to his mother. But poor boy he can't form any sentences so he just making noise. Debby know is something wrong so she quarrelling and you could hear she voice from quite down in the junction, because she mouth loud plus she voice squeaky. The workers don't pay no mind to Debby; they just ignore her and continue with dey business. But, when she becomes overbearing they does ask her to shut up and Debby does vex. Sometimes she does cry and say she wants to go home. But from what I hear others saying, Debby ent have no home so she have to remain in the shelter. She in the shelter the longest—she dey seven years—seven long years.

The home does smell like stale pee and sometimes I does not want to eat the food, especially if is dumpling or homemade bread. The scent makes me sick at times; it does raise me sinus and cause me to sneeze. And when I sneeze everybody does laugh because they does say me sneeze sounding kicksy.

I could hear them bus passing—some going towards Sauteurs and some going to Grenville. We were not allowed to leave the compound so I does just sit down in the back of the house and watch and imagine things. I does watch the birds feeding on the cherry and the lizards running up and down. Sometimes I does watch the old man who always planting things in the bottom of the hill -the way he does bend his back as he cut the grass and the way he uses his dirty hands to wipe the sweat on he face. Sometimes I does see him untying the bottle from his waist and he does bend he head and drink the water.

I does think a lot about the good times that I use to enjoy before Uncle Jack started having sex with me; the times I would go fishing in the river, digging below father's nutmeg tree to find the earthworms I used for bait, and searching through the bushes to find coconut to use for husks. The coconut husks does make the crayfish come out and it makes fishing a whole lot easier. I don't like catching 'sovet' because they too small. I rather hold 'reds' and 'ling'. Sometimes Jim, my little brother, used to come with me, but he always talking and he does run the crayfish.

I miss playing with my neighbours too. We use to make wicket and play cricket in the road and when a vehicle coming we rushing to remove it and go on the side for them to pass. I don't like when I out; I does feel to take the wicket and throw it in the bush. Mama say that's not a good way and sometimes when Elisa go and complain Mama does come up in the road and curse and tell me come inside. But my team does always win because when we throw head or tail we always get to win and we does pick first and Tasha does choose the best players. We does play moral and hopscotch too and sometimes we does play dodge the ball. I don't like dodge the ball because one time I fall down and burst me lip and Mama say the burst lip take away from me beauty because it leave a big growing flesh on me bottom lip.

When school on break we does sit down under the street light and tell jumbie stories. Scary, scary stories about La Diablesse and Mama Malady, and me skin does raise because them jumbie stories real scary. Once upon a time they say a man was coming from the garden. It was late and he was walking all by himself - just him and God. When he reach Flaming turning, he see a tall, tall man and when the man grin he had plenty, plenty teeth and he face scary. So he run until he reach the junction. When he reach the junction he see another man and the man ask him.

"Why you running so?"

"I now see a tall, tall man and the man have plenty, plenty teeth".

They say the man look at him, open he mouth and asked, "Teeth like these?"

Dey say the man cudda mess he self because he was now talking to the jumbie.

They say La Diablesse use to go in dance and dress pretty, pretty. They have one cow foot and one human foot. And after the dance most of the men does want to take them home because of they charm and beauty.

"Michelle, it's time to come in!" I heard someone shout— breaking my thoughts and disturbing my concentration. I stood up, put my slippers on my feet and walk towards the house—that stupid boring home that made everything seem dead and unhappy.

Chapter 27: Summoned

Miss Mitchell told me she had a summons. Summons is ah thing they does

send when you have to go in the court house—the court house wey cousin

Hannah does always go and sit down to mind people business. Cousin

Hannah always know who going in jail, who thief, who kill and who rape

because she does live in the people court house. Dedra say Hannah too fast

and that they must lock her up for she forwardness, because she have no right to be going and sit down in the court house everyday.

Ms Mitchell told me that the case with me and my stepfather starting so I have to go and give evidence. The court is the next day so she told me I must be brave and ready to speak, I looked at her and shook me head. Of course I brave and I ready to speak because I want justice. Everybody saying I lie so is my only chance to prove them wrong.

The children in school does tease me. They say I is a wicked girl and I does take me stepfather. One of my good friends stop talk to me; she say she mother tell her to stay far, far away from me; that I was a whore and I will influence her. So these days I does just stay for myself. I don't really feel like going to school anymore because everybody does treat me different and when I passing people does be casting remarks, especially the older girls. They tell me my 'cun cun' big and it tear up and no man ent want me and me and me mother does take same man. One time ah girl tell me that and when I complain to Miss Black she tell me get out ah she office that she ent want to hear; she doh know why I doh leave school.

So anybody tell me anything I does curse them real bad, because I don't care anymore; half of my life done gone and I don't really business about the rest. I does curse them teachers too and they does ask me to come out of they class. Ah does refuse to go and they does go and call the principal. Ramlogan don't come but Black will come with her old stupid voice and start to get on and curse me and tell me all kind ah thing. I does answer her back and tell her all she could do is just talk because if she hit me ah hitting her back and even if she suspend me, she can't suspend me forever.

Chapter 28: Court Case

Ah ent really fraid but I kinda nervous; ah doh know what it like going in

ah court house. All I know is that when you go court house you does go in

jail and our pastor say it's not good to go in the court house anyway. Plus I

don't want to go to jail, and they say the judge is ah rough man, the one in

Grenville. They say the man real heartless and wicked; he doh make no joke

when it come to the law. Ah hear Troy say the judge once asked a man to go outside and count how much vehicles he see. The man go and count and

when he come back he say twenty. Troy say the judge tell the man take

twenty years in jail. Ah doh know if Troy was joking or serious, if he lying or

he telling the truth. Ah just saying after him.

Ah put on me school clothes and I watch myself in the mirror -the plait
and twist in me hair still neat. Ah does plait me hair for myself because I
don't want to sit down in front nobody. Ah getting ah little bit fair and I
getting fat too. Me jaw ent looking hard as the devil padlock again; it getting
fat and when I smile my cheeks looking fat too.

I still doh like the home but I get accustom to it and I settle down ah little.
Ah eating now and I'm helping with chores. Miss Mitchell does teach me to
crochet and I trying to make a nice tablecloth to give her as a present. I does
spend plenty time in me Bible now and I does pray ah lot too and on
Saturdays when I ent tired I does go to church up in St Patrick, up that big
hill that does bend me back when ah walking like Plaisance own.

Nobody still ent coming to visit me, but I don't care. I get accustom with
that too. But sometimes I does remember everything and I does cry plenty; I
does feel depressed, heart broken and alone. But Psalm thirty-seven does
comfort me. It's my favourite scripture: Fret not thyself because of evildoers.

I continued looking at myself in the mirror while waiting for the ministry van to pick us up People say I pretty but I doh really see it. They say me nose straight as me mother own and we look alike that's why we can't agree. It's not that we can't agree. Mama just don't like me, plus Mama kinda fair and I black like a Congo; so I don't know how people does be saying that we look alike.

I heard a horn blow and a vehicle pulled up. I grabbed my bag, looked in the mirror, smiled at myself and walked out the door. I walked towards Miss Mitchell's office but she was not dey. They say somebody had to accompany me, so Miss Grace decided to come. When I walked in the verandah she was outside waiting. She was dressed real nice—her Rasta hair up in one and she was wearing ah suit and smelling good too. Sometimes I does want to beg her for some perfume but Mama say it ent good to beg—she say when you beg man, they does go with you and they does give you more than what you beg for.

The van pulled up in front the courthouse, just on the side of the market wey them St David bus does park up to get passengers. Early morning but Grenville full up ah people ah ready. I walked out of the van and grab Miss Grace's hand. Ah kinda shame and frighten; ah thinking about the things people saying about me.

From the corner of my eyes, I saw people staring and pointing they fingers, some even putting they hands on they head, which is a sign of disgrace; others looked at me and laughed. Ah see a woman point at me, spit on the ground and looked away just as she was about to trample the spit with her foot. There was an urge inside me to just run - run as fast as I could, but I had no idea as to where I was going to run to. So I just grip Miss Grace tighter and walk towards the court.

The courthouse is a real old building; the paint and everything looking like it tired and ready to just fall down and dead. In fact the whole building looking like it dead ah ready. To get to the courthouse it have about two steps you have to climb and the step always full ah people. Most of them ent have no matters in the court you know, they just fast and like to mind people business.

We walked pass them and head inside the building. We passed the policeman standing in front the door and went straight inside.

Outside don't look too nice but inside the room real nice and pretty. The benches polished too and it have a big glass thing close to wey the judge sit down. The benches and them full up and the only space it had available is ah seat in the back. Ah look around and ah see cousin Hannah; they ent lie in truth, she always dey.

The judge called out the matters and the policeman shouted out the names on the top of his voice. My case ent call yet so I sit down listening. A man got charged for stealing two watermelons and some batteries. The judge ask him how he plead and he say "guilty." He say he take the battery to listen cricket and that he had plans on returning it. The judge look at him, shake he head and tell him to pay the court eight hundred dollars.

My case was called, but just before, they walked in with Uncle Jack with handcuffs on his hand. He was wearing a blue pants and a blue shirt and his shirt stick down in his pants. Uncle Jack turned back and look at me and I grab back Miss Grace hand. I see Mama too, but Miss Grace tell me don't look at her, so I obeyed.

They asked that the court be cleared and everybody went outside- well everyone except me, Mama, Uncle Jack, Miss Grace and a lady dress in all black. I later found out that the lady in black was a lawyer that was hired to represent the monster.

The judge called my name and I said present. They called Uncle Jack's name and he say, "Yes your honour."

"Come forward Miss Alexander."

I walked towards the front of the court with Miss Grace by my side. I was frightened and trying my best not to let it show

"Do you know this man standing in front of me?" the judge asked.

"Yes." I answered.

"What is he to you?" the judge continued.

"My stepfather," I said, looking at him straight in his eyes. He looked at me too and I realised I was not scared.

"Your honour, on behalf of my client I will like to ask this young lady a few questions." It was the lady in black—the short fair skinned lady that had walked in earlier with a briefcase.

"You may proceed," the judge said. She turned around to look at me.

"Sabrena, you said that the man standing before you is your stepfather?"

"Yes."

"He used to punish you?"

"Yes, because Uncle Jack used to beat me when I did bad things; he used to try and correct me, but he used to have sex with me and that was wrong."

"So because he does punish you is that why you saying he raped you?"

What kind of stupid, dottish question was she asking me? I looked at her, then I looked at Mama and then I looked at Uncle Jack.

"If somebody punishing you, you would say they rape you?" I asked with tears running down my cheeks.

"You are not allowed to ask me questions," she hissed.

"Your honour, all that we have on our hand is just a rebellious child, trying to escape punishment according to that child"s mother." She was pointing at Mama now.

"The only reason she's making this claim is because she was punished by her stepfather. This is nothing but a rebellious act. My client is innocent."

I was becoming angry. Why was she referring to me as a liar? Was she there?

"I'm not lying Sir and this is not about punishment. Uncle Jack did have sex with me and there's nothing to lie about." I was crying and Miss Grace was rubbing my shoulder.

The judge and the lawyer continued talking and with each word I kept getting more and more angry. After about ten minutes later, the judge said that he was remanding Uncle Jack and transferring the matter to the high court. As soon as Mama hear that she started bawling again.

"Oh god, oh god me husband! he innocent! he innocent! let go me husband. Allu can't send him back to jail!"

Ah looked at Mama and the most I could of done was just shake me head. The woman ent even care about how I feeling and that made me kinda feel bad. Mama eyes full up ah tears but she ent crying for me; she crying for she husband.

Chapter 29: Sad News

I returned to the home with a heavy heart. It was still kinda impossible for

me to believe the wickedness of my mother. So I just sat there, lost in

thought, wishing my life was different. Later during the day I was told to

pack my things because they were transferring me to another home. They say

the home they were going to put me in now was suitable for me since it had

girls my age. I don't know why they were moving me when I done get comfortable with Mangroves although some of the staff does tell me mean

things—they say I'm damaged goods that's why nobody ent want me. But I

get use to them and I could care less about what anybody say. And me and

Debby is good friends too; she does tell me a lot of nice stories and she does

make me read the Bible for her. So I go miss Debby and I go miss crazy

Denna too, because Denna does make me laugh—she does do a lot ah funny

things.

Ah time Denna pack she bag to go. After Denna reach by the gate, she come back and say she ent going again because she now get a phone call and they say the house burn down. Denna ent even have a phone. I laugh so hard that day, I almost pee me self. Every time I see Denna I does remember the joke so I does always laugh and Denna don't know what I laughing at, but she does be laughing too.

I packed my bag. I don't have much things to pack, because I don't have plenty clothes. Miss Mitchell say she go miss me and I go miss her too because she is a nice lady and she does bring a lot ah nice things for me. She does teach me plenty handycraft too- not just crocheting- she does teach me to make chains and earrings using beads. She took out a chain in her neck and gave me.

"Take care of it and take care of you," she said as she kissed me on my cheek.

I smiled and looked up at her. "Yes, yes," I assured her.

But deep down inside I don't want to leave; I don't know how the other place go be.

"Miss Mitchell, you dropping me?"

"No, somebody from Social Services coming for you."

"But why?" I asked, as the tears were forming in the corner ah me eyes and me voice sounding hoarse, hoarse as if I swallow a frog.

"Doh worry chile, it go be alright and you go like it there. You go have more people to play with; they ent boring as Mangroves."

"But here ent boring." I said, "I does make beads and crochet with you and Debby and them does keep me company. Is not everybody here bad."

"Listen," she say and she put me on her lap.

"Here is nice, it's not boring but it's not the place for you. You is a child and here is for women—women that was abused by their husbands; women that could be your mother. So as much as you don't want to go you have to because this environment is not the best for you. You need to be a child and do children things. Here is not children-friendly. You understand?"

"Yes," I said, and buried my head in her bosom. Out of the many bad staff, she was one of the good ones. She knew better than me so maybe what she saying is the right thing.

Chapter 30: Sexual Abuse Shelter

When they brought me in the sexual abuse shelter, it was already late. They

had me sit down in child protection services without even offering me

something to eat and I was upset. Why the hell they had to make me sit down

all these hours?

The sexual abuse shelter was different from Mangroves. It's not as big and it's a flat building, Mangroves big and the building tall. But this one just flat. It fence around like Mangroves but there's no security and it have plenty fruit trees. Although it' was night, I saw a mango and ah orange tree. I love mango - it's my favourite fruit.

We walked through the gate, entered the veranda and passed through a door that led to an open hall. I was introduced to the staff and one by one I was introduced to the residents- the other girls who like myself was being abused and had nowhere to stay. There were familiar faces—girls I had known from the Sapodilla Home and they were happy to see me, but I was not happy to see them.

After the introduction, I followed one of the caretakers up the wooden stairs and into another hallway that led to a big room. There were two corridors, but we took the one on the right. There were plenty bunk beds inside—at least ten, and I was given one, as well as a locker to store my clothes.

"Put away you things and come for dinner." The woman talking to me was a nice woman and she was pretty too. She was introduced as Miss Sara and she was smiling at me. I smiled back at her and she winked her eyes and walked away.

The room was empty because the girls were outside. I looked around wondering if all the beds in the room was occupied and wondered which of the girls I would be sharing with.

I was unpacking my bags looking for one of my Nancy Drew books that I had the intention of finishing. I love Nancy Drew books and my mother liked them too. My brother had bought me ten from his last visit in America and I enjoyed reading each and every one of them. The mysteries were intriguing and Nancy was a brave girl. I dared to be brave as Nancy, because she was my role model. She is a strong girl too and she's smart because she always gets away from the bad things she had to face.

Then I heard my name called. So I quickly turned around. It was one of the girls from the Sapodilla Home—Alana. I rest down the bag and looked up at Alana wondering why she disturbing me. She was wearing a red dress and she had on blue slippers on her feet—feet that were covered with bruises. She stood on the side of the bed with her hands on her waist and she was looking at me straight in my eyes—poor me one, poor me one.

"What you doing here?" she asked.

"The same thing you doing here," I replied.

"Aw Sabrena, how you getting on so?"

Was she expecting me to explain my reason for being here?

"Here nice?" I asked trying to change the topic.

Alana walked towards me and without an invitation she sat down on the bed.

"Here ent really nice; they does treat us bad and most of the girls does run away," she whispered

I raised up my head and looked at her.

"Runaway?"

"Yes," she said.

"But why?"

Before Alana could answer we were interrupted. Another girl walked in the room. She looked at Alana up and down, stupsed and walked towards one of the beds in the corner.

"Sabrena ah going. My room is on the other side if you want you could come over."

Alana gone and I still wondering what she mean by runaway.What Alana talking about? After I was finished unpacking, I joined the others in living room.

Chapter 31: Pussy Cat

I got up and told everyone good morning. I walked inside the locker, got my

devotional book and searched through the pages. When I found what I was

looking for, I read it in my mind. Then I whispered my prayers. I does always

read my devotional book—that's how I always start my day. Then I prayed

asking God for wisdom, knowledge and understanding. I also asked Him to

protect me and to guide me and give me strength to face all the challenges that life has to offer. And when I pray I does feel much better until something

else happen to tip me off and remind me of my pain.

I smelled the oven bread that Miss Moore was baking and my belly rumbled with hunger. Mama say for a little magga girl I too darn greedy and I does act as if the banana boat passing through me belly because I could never satisfy. You should see the small bowl Mama use to feed people in. And is plenty small bowls and sometimes it does have extra bowls for she friend's children too. So I must always hungry; I ent have no bird stomach.

Sometime I find they does take too long to feed us, I smelled the porridge boiling. Farine had a special scent—it was like smoke herring, always bringing news.

"Sabrena you want to play a game?" Frances asked me with dribble running down she mouth and wax in her eye.

I looked at Frances. I liked playing games, but I wondering if Frances know what time it is- people just get up. Me doh even brush the stinkness out me mouth yet and Frances asking me if I want to play game. Like Frances not feeling the 'ka-ka-jay' in her eyes that need cleaning.

"It too early for that," I said and I continued reading.

Frances looked at me with a disappointed look on she face and she doing as if she want to cry, but it too early in truth; nobody ent going and play game this hour.

Mornings at the home does normally be loud and crazy because is plenty girls and whereever you have females is always plenty confusion. Somebody always blaming somebody else for something and they always accusing each other for stealing.

Once I missed my nice gold watch—ah gold watch my godmother gave me as a present since I was a little girl and I does cherish it because it's a special gift. I took it out one day, put it down on my bunk and when I come back the watch tell me if I could see it take it. I look up, down and around but I ent see me watch and all who I asked, everybody saying they don't know. I made a report to the manager and they called a search and looked in everyone belongings, but all the look they look we still ent find the watch.

One day when I went to school, I saw Jason with a watch looking just like mines. I know my watch so I asked Jason to see it. It have the same scrape on the face and one of the loops missing the same place wey mines missing. I asked Jason how he get the watch and he tell me his girlfriend gave him. When I asked who is his girlfriend he say Chandelle. Chandelle is one of the girls in the home. So Chandelle is the one who took the watch and she is the same one that was helping me look for it. She was searching all under the bed, digging up and emptying everything. I know I was not leaving Jason with me watch. Ah want it. That watch very, very special to me. I asked him for it and he tell me he not giving me. I decided not to wild him. When I reach home I will deal with Miss Chandelle.

That evening I got home early and I sat down on the veranda waiting on Chandelle. I spot her as she dropped off the bus, modelling coming up the dirt track. She walking and swaying she body for them boys to see because she have a nice figure and a pretty face too. She pretty, pretty, but I never guess one day that the girl was a pussy cat. She does always talk about how she mother in America and how much nice things she mother does send for her. She does always say how much she mother love her and I does want to ask her what mother who loves her child would put her and leave her in a home. But I does hush me mouth because I don't want to make nobody feel bad, because I don't like it when others make me feel bad.

She opened the gate and walked in. That gate always making noise; they say the hinges rusty but nobody ent fixing it.

"Michelle what you doing in the veranda?" Chandelle asked. Chandelle have a nice voice; not a hoarse voice as Alana, and she could sing too.

"I'm waiting for you," I said, running my hand through me picky hair that refused to grow.

"You waiting fah me? Wah you waiting for me fah? Ah owe you?"

"Yes." I was still running my hands through my hair.

"I want to know what you do with me watch."

Chandelle whole mood changed; her red face was starting to get purple and she started stamping she foot.

"Y-yo-you." Ah never hear her stammer but she stammering now for me and I wondering if is stupid she playing.

"Me watch girl and doh stammer for me!"

Chandelle walked closer toward me.

"Hush, hush, doh talk loud," resting she hand on my shoulder.

"I'll be punished if they find out."

"So is you take it eh? because is yours ent?"

"Yes, but shhhhh."

"But why you never think about being punished before? Why you take it in the first place? And to make things even worse you was helping me look for it. Girl, you is ah real dread thief."

"Ah go give you me bag, the nice brown polka dot one and I go get back the watch Friday."

I smiled, but not big enough to show it. She had a bag I liked in truth and I really wanted it, especially where bus trip was coming up.

"Yes, ah go take it but make sure I get me watch, because if I doh get it you won't like what go happen to you."

She shook her head in agreement and walked towards the door; then she disappeared in the building.

The evening breeze hit me face and I smiled. Chandelle was really going to give me she polka dot bag. So it was a good thing she thief me watch. Then and I wondered how long it was going to be before she thief something again.

Chapter 32: My First Fight

I was still going to school in Grenville. They were thinking about getting

a transfer for me to go in one of the schools in town but that ent come

through as yet. I does have to get up really early because my school is the

farthest and before I leave for school I does have to complete my chores.

Sometimes I does have to sweep the whole yard and pick up all the leaves. I

does have to wash down the yard too, especially when it rains and the mud goes on the concrete. Other times I does have to do the dishes or clean our

room. But I does work fast and sometimes I does get tokens and privileges

for being obedient and completing my chores. Some of the privileges

included using the computer or going with the staff in the grocery, I don't

really beat up about the computer because I ent know nothing much about it.

We school have computers, but I can't stand that coolie man so whenever is

time for his class, I does go behind the school and sit down with my friends who ent want school like me. To say I doh like the man is ah understatement.

I can't stand the best bone in him. So yes I does rather go in the grocery or on

the beach. Not me on computer papa; what donkey know about using

Colgate?

From Mt Parnasus to Grenville is a far distance and ah lot ah ride. This is something I don't like because I does feel to vomit, especially when the bus going over Grand Etang—that cold, misty place that full ah trees and monkeys, and the road an'd dem narrow, narrow. When dem bus passing it does look like they want to drive down the precipice. Whenever them bus going over there I does say me prayers because I don't want to die; ah want to get old like Miss Mary. Before I used to think children never died, but after Jim (ah boy that was in Grade Five in Munich) died, my thinking changed and every night before I go to sleep I will pray and ask God to bless me to see old age. Mama say is wicked people that does live for long. Ah don't get worried at all for Mama, because I know she have long, long to live.

The home have rules; you does have to be there by a certain hour. They give me up to four o'clock, but I does reach home by three-thirty and even though all them other girls' school is in town, I does still reach home before them and my school way up behind God's back in the country. When we gather in the night for meetings and devotion some of the staff does ask them rest ah girls why they can't be like me and come home early. Some of them being rude usually give back answers and some of them does curse too.

Mostly everybody in the home have a boyfriend, but me I never even had a boyfriend. I don't have time for that- maybe when I get older. And they does be talking in the room about who booming who and how they does boom they boyfriend. One of the girls' boyfriend living next door and when everybody sleeping she does sneak out and go by him. They does punish her but she doh care.

Once they send me in the shop and when I went, a boy talked to me. He asked me my name but I was not taking him on. They had sent me together with Don to get some yeast so that the cook could bake some bread. The boy kept harassing me and I kept avoiding him. He told Don to set him up on her friend and Don said, yes. Little did I know Lenna liked the same boy. So when I reach back home, to my greatest surprise, Lenna come and confront me, asking me what I want with she man and how Don tell her he was confronting me. At first I thought it was a joke but when the girl pushed me, I realise she was serious. My back bounce the bed iron and I tried to break my fall by shifting my feet.

I shook my head wondering to myself if that girl really knew what she was doing. It was true I hardly talk and I walked around playing stupidy, but my death was for people to touch me; to raise their filthy hand and hit me.

"Lenna you know what you doing, you really know what you doing?" I asked. There were other girls in the room. Most of them were Lenna's friends and they were sending body languages to Lenna urging her to beat me up and hit me again. Lenna pushed me again, but this time I stood firm and my body did not bounce the bed iron. I stretched out my hand, grabbing Lena by her collar and spinned her around and knock her down on the bed. Then I jumped on her without warning and started punching her in she face- she face rough like frog back but I don't care. I punching her still and something keep telling me to go in me bag and get my razor blade and chop Lenna in her face. Lenna tried fighting back but the way I pinned her down she wasn't able to move and now that I realised I had the advantage, I was hitting her real hard.

The next thing I felt was someone pulling me. When I looked around it was one of the care takers,

"You and Lenna follow me to the office."

I walked behind her, me face puff up like if I want to explode and most of the girls laughing at Lenna as she bend she head in shame.When we reached the office, the caretaker locked the door and she looked at both of us.

"Michelle, you, this good for nothing child, if you know how much I don't like you. No wonder you stepfather use to boom you up. You think you better than everybody eh? Acting as if you is this decent child. Everybody in here is little whores; is long I want to tell you, but is only now I get the chance. You not a virgin; you is damaged goods. So stop acting as if you better than any of the other residents."

I looked up at Miss Brandy and anger shot through my body. Immediately I got a headache, mixed with rage and emotions. Before I knew it tears were running down my cheeks. She called me a whore.I looked at her. She was sitting on the desk with her foot folded and the piece of skirt she was wearing was riding up her legs. I had so much emotions running through me that I was trembling.

"Shut up!" she yelled. "You always putting tears in front. You wicked child. Coming to think of it, I wonder if your stepfather really boom you or is just one of you wicked acts."

I felt my throat go dry and something touch the corner of my head. I felt a sudden pain in between my legs too; it was the pain I always felt before Uncle Jack made me open my legs very wide, before penetrating me. I felt his hands too moving over my body and I smelt his scent. Everything was coming back to me—everything, and I was becoming angrier and angrier.

"You want to know wey the whore is?" Without waiting for a reply I continued, "The whore they in you mother stinking dirty rotten front." I was not only angry I was hurting. She sprang from the chair, grabbed me in my collar and slammed me against the door. Pain shot through my body as my head knocked against the knob and I cried out in pain. Lenna was looking on and laughing at me.

Chapter 33: Under The Mango Tree

I pushed open the door angrily and I ran outside to the living room. Tears

were running down my cheeks and I felt bad inside. Why did she say all these

to me? Why did she have to remind me of the past and most of all why did

she call me a liar?

Being called a liar was the thing that made me angry the most, because even Mama called me a liar. The woman who went through so much pain to make me and who was still trying to make my life a living hell. All in school Mama was coming and trying to make things bad for me. Mama told people how I nasty and I this and I that and how I use to leave she house and go and take man. I does feel to get a big, big piece ah wood and just knock down Mama; hit her all in her head. If Mama only know how much I can't stand her. Sometimes I does even pray for her to dead. But God have a way of not answering some of my prayers. Not all because sometimes He does answer some. I have no respect for the woman, no respect at all and I don't like her. So whenever she see me and she curse me I does curse her back. I don't curse her under my throat the way I used to when I use to live in her house, I cursing her loud, because I want her to hear everything that I saying. She does tell me things and I does tell her things too. Some people does say I go catch curse because I don't have respect for me mother and how I'm not a good child and I won't reach no way in life. I don't really know what that mean but I does tell them, *wey horse reach donkey must reach too.* Why must I respect somebody who ent respect me? Make it worse she say I is not she child so I cursing her back because I don't care, nor can I catch curse twice because the amount ah curse Mama done put on me ah ready.

But I still wondering what right the woman have to tell me all that. I still crying and I feeling to just go in the kitchen, get a knife and stab her up. Stab her until she take her last breath. That's how mad I does get especially when people tell me I am lying on me stepfather knowing fully well what I had to endure and still enduring because of that wicked piece ah garbage that call himself a man.

I run out the living room, almost tripping over the mop and went below the mango tree. Whenever I feel upset I does go and sit down under the mango tree. I does sit on the bare ground and I does brace me back on the tree stump. I does bury my head in my lap and I does cry bitterly. I remember so many things and I does get depressed. It does feel like if the whole world is on my shoulder but I does be helpless because I can't do nothing about it.

I does wonder if God love me and even if He love me, why he putting me through all these things. Why I have to be in a home and why my stepfather had to boom me, after how much I had looked up to him. Why everybody make me go and why do I have to be in a place wey people ent like me and wey some of the staff does tell me mean and hurtful things and having to face punishment when I answer back.

I does really get upset and sad and sometimes I does cut me hands. I have a pack ah razor blade I bought in the supermarket. It does hurt but seeing the blood oozing from my hand does make me feel a little better. They say when I feel like that I must count to ten or think of a safe place. A safe place? I don't think it have any safe place in Grenada or on the face of the earth, so I don't even bother wasting my time.

Something about nature does make me feel better. I don't know if it's the singing of the birds, the way the wind blows and touch me face, being surrounded by trees or if is just being beneath the naked skies.

"Sabrena you okay?" I removed my head from my laps and looked up. It was Alana. Oh God that girl again! I looked at her, unable to say a word and she looked back at me. There was a look of pity and concern in her eyes.

"I sitting down by you eh," she said.

I allowed her to sit and I continued crying. My body was shaking too and I was tapping my fingers on the ground. I was really, really upset. Alana moved closer to me and she took my hands inside hers.

"I does cry too Sabrena. As I tell you, here ent nice, but you does have to be strong; you does have to have a mind of you own and you does have to desire better for youself. That's what they do here. They make you feel bad. I does want to run away too but it's better for me if I stay here because I don't really have no way to go."

"But why they have to be like that? Just imagine Lenna is the one that interfered with me, and she ent tell Lenna nothing but she call me a whore and push me on the door."

"She told you that?" Alana asked with her squeaky voice that does sound like if she crying.

"Yes."

"Hmmm, Lenna is one of they favourites eh; they does normally take up for her and you know the funny thing, when they do us bad things and we complain, it makes matters worse because they does say we lying. And whenever the people from child protection leave, we does be punished, so it ent have much we could possibly do. All I can tell you is to be strong and hold on. Better go come one day." I told Alana I'll be leaving soon because my father supposed to come and get me.

Chapter 34: Good News

Sometimes I does wonder what crime I commit to be going through all these things. They say people who have curse that does see trouble so. But what curse I could have at this tender age? I ent do nobody nothing. Why I have to suffer so much? Me family big. I have so many aunties, uncles, brothers, sisters; so much cousins and yet still is like I'm alone. People does tell me is wicked, I wicked that's why me mother make me go and I have to be in a home. I does cry and I does want to kill myself. I does just feel to buy some

gramoxone and drink it. Dey say when you kill youself you does go in hell,

but is like ah dey in hell ah ready, because if hell is more than what I going

through then hell have to be a real bad place.

Them staff does call me all kinda names too. They say I'm damaged goods and no man won't want me because below me juck up like yam bed and manicou nest. I know what a manicou nest look like and I know for sure below me ent looking like that. But whenever they tell me that, I does cry and I does feel real bad too and when I answer them they does punish me. They does wait until Miss Jacky ent dey and sometimes they don't give me food to eat either. They say I must eat me finger nails.

Ah does wonder if some ah dem have girl children and if they will like for people to tell they girl children that and treat them so. I does remember Mama words too about how man go take me all over the face ah the earth and how I black and ugly like a Congo. Ah does wonder why Mama never had an abortion; why the hell she had to bring me in this world for; why she had to make me and let me see all this trouble.

Them workers in the home say I dunce too and they don't know why the government still wasting they money to send me to school. I does come last in test but that's not what I want to come. I coming last because I does find it hard to focus. When is time for class ah lot ah things does be running through my mind so I can't focus. When is time to write the exam I does remember what Mama tell me, how I won't reach no way in life so I does just rest down me head and wait until the bell ring and hand up the paper when the time up. Mama know better than me and if she say ah won't reach any way then I won't reach any way; so it ent make no sense ah fight up. So I does just settle for the last position without putting in any effort. Everybody can't come first and besides nobody in me family ever reach in Form Four so that alone is ah accomplishment. At least I dunce but I moving up in class. But I was not always dunce. In Form Two I came second. I beat ah lot ah children. When I get the report book and the teacher say I come second, she was shocked and wondered how in God's earth that was possible.

One day I came home from school and I got the good news—I was moving out to live with my new parents in Carriacou. When God cannot come He surely will send someone because I was beginning to get fed up with them in that home and I know if they had continued, I was going to lose my temper and damage one ah them.

Chapter 35: New Beginnings

Daddy and Mom were both debating as to whether I should go Bishop's

College or Hillsborough Secondary. I had a new home because I was now

living with Daddy and my stepmother. Daddy's house have more things than

Mama own. It have inside bathroom, stove, fridge, running water, telephone,

computer and Daddy have internet too. Everybody have a room and a bed

and nobody ent have to sleep on the floor. In the night nobody doh have to fight with me for me bed and ah like that.

I wasn't in Grenada anymore. I was in Carriacou. I went with the big boat- the one that does make plenty noise and spend hours on the sea. Carriacou is a rather beautiful place; the beaches are wonderful. It is not like the rough dirty water in Gouyave wey my brother does bring me to bathe. Sometimes he would take me out on his fishing boat and I would even get to drive it. My brother is my favourite person. I love him real bad.

To reach Carriacou, you have to take a boat or the small plane. It have a beach right behind the house and the water is crystal clear.It have plenty grapes on that beach-sweet, sweet grapes that I does go and pick and full me belly.

So they finally decided that I should go Bishop's College— that's the school I want to go to anyway because I hear it is the better school. They got me accepted and I got my school uniform. Nice school uniform—not like Grenville Secondary and they straight grey skirt. This one is a pleated skirt-same color like St Andrews Anglican Secondary and the color of the tie look like they own too; the whole uniform in fact. The only difference is that Bishop's College shoes black and St Andrews Anglican is white.

The morning before school I was all excited. I felt brand new and for the first time in my life wanted to learn; I wanted to make use of all opportunities and I wanted to make a difference. I didn't want to place last as how I was placing in my former school. I didn't want to continue failing. I wanted to pass all my subjects and I wanted to go to college. I was in Form Four and I have just one year to get my act together. I had faith and I believe I could do it once I apply myself in the right way.

Daddy bought all my books and he said I must always think and be positive. He said I'm the one in charge of my destiny and it's only me to make the difference. Nobody can make that difference for me.

I was fifteen and ah put me hair in bubbles and clip -plenty bubbles and plenty clips. Mom plait my hair and I put on me uniform and I was looking very, very neat and nice too. The only thing I didn't like was my bag. It have too much pocket and it looks like a parachute.

At school, I met a nice handsome boy who got me my table and chair and he put it in the corner by the window, just after the first row, and he put his table next to mine. He told me his name and smiled at me and I smiled back.

Most of the children friendly and I don't know if it's only because I'm the new girl. Every time ah new teacher come into the class I have to stand up and introduce myself. They made the students introduce themselves too so I can remember their names. There is another girl with the same name like mine but she red and I am black and when we keep mixing up who they were calling, a girl said "Red Michelle" not "Black Michelle" and they laughed.

My first day of school was not bad; I made some new friends—Nicole and Clara. Franko and Jeremy are my friends too but I already know them because all of us living in L'Esterre. Nicole was the person who took me around and showed me everything. She showed me the tuck shop and told me how much for the food. She also took me to the computer lab and upstairs to the different classrooms. Nicole was showing me everything and me and her laughing like we know each other long, long, long.

Nicole was slim and pretty, with long hair and a straight nose. She told me the principal is her aunty but she don't act like it. I ent see Nicole go by she aunty for the day. In GSS when you had a relative who was a teacher, the children use to be all under they crotch, but Nicole was different; she not doing that and if she didn't tell me ah woulda never guess.

I does play quiet and sometimes I hardly talk. About three weeks into the term, one day whilst going upstairs the corridor, I was confronted by three girls; they were considered to be the school bullies, but me I ent fraid ah nobody. They corner me and I just stand there looking at them. They all taller than me and they fat too; they ent too good looking either.

Earlier in Religious Instruction class I had clashed with one of them. The teacher had asked a question and they tried to answer but they were wrong. Then she asked me and I answered it correctly. So because of that, the girl got vex and started watching me bad eyes and showing me kill sign. I answered her and told her to keep she threats to herself. We started throwing chat at each other and Miss told us to stop. So I stopped, but the girl continued.

"Yes, Misss know it all," said one of them looking down at

me. I looked up at her, she big nose spread across she face like the rash you does catch when you play with dirty water. I ent saying ah word but I watching her, straight in she eyes and she and her friends watching me too.

"So you didn't think we woulda catch you," the fat one with the cow breast said. She breast dey like it want to burst she shirt and run from she chest and she hair picky, picky. I could smell she perspiration too. Some of these things running through me mind. Ah wondering why she doh go and address she arm instead of blocking me.

"If allu know what good for allu, move let me pass eh." Me hand on me waist and I shaking me frame. I was stomping me foot on the ground and it sounding like a rhythm.

"Move let you pass to go way?"

"To go about me business. Allu think people fraid allu. Tell me why allu blocking me. Allu think I scared ah allu right? But know that I ent fraid ah soul and allu could stand dey as long as allu want to, say what allu want to, do what allu want to, but just doh let allu shadow bounce me, because if allu shadow only rush me allu won't like the end result."

I pushed my way through them and walked away. They just stood there looking at me. As I walked down the corridor, I felt their eyes cutting through my back. But that was all they could have done because if they had only touched me I was going to touch them back and all hell would have broken loose.

Chapter 36: Dear Diary

Some people does see me as a happy child, because I always laughing but

none of them know what I really going through. Sometimes I does miss

Mama and I does miss my brothers and sisters too. If I could control time I

would have surely gone back and changed everything. But I can't do that so I

have to live with the pain in me heart- the pain I wished would go away.

I does try not to remember what Uncle Jack did to me, but whenever I am by myself everything does come back and I get scared and sad all over again. I remember his hairy hands touching my skin, his breath on my neck, his scent of coconut oil, the evil look in his eyes and the way he slammed me on the cold floor.

I does lock my door and cry plenty too. I would feel as if my soul leaving my body the same way I does feel when Uncle Jack forcing his shaft inside me. I would feel the tears forming in the back ah me eyes and before I could check myself water running down me face. People does say ah easy to cry, but dey ent even know half of my life story and what I going through. Nobody in Carriacou know I was raped, not even me brothers and sisters. I feel real, real sad -the same way I does feel if Christmas come and I ent get a toy.

Outside done dark ah ready, but was me alone at home. Mom ent come from work yet and even if mom was home I would still be in my room. She ent really like me;she does move funny. Sometimes when I say morning she does answer me down in her throat or she might just fling she hand in recognition.

I turned on my bed and put on the light switch and searched through my going out clothes for me diary. I have a diary with a padlock and key and the cover has a pretty mermaid. The mermaid's face is covered with glittering dust and when the sun hot the glitter does want to blind you eyes because it bright, bright, bright. I does always hide it and even though it have a key, I hiding it still because is all kinda thing I have inside there, including the name of the boy that I like. I don't want nobody, not even Daddy to see me business. My diary have a pen too. The diary looked happy to see me and I was happy to see it too, because I don't know the last day I wrote in it. I unlocked the padlock, picked up me pen and I sat down on my bed.

Dear Diary,

Ah know it's been long I never write to you. I'm no longer in the home so I don't have to complain to you about people stealing my stuff and the workers calling me names. I'm in Carriacou now. Carriacou is nice and it have some real nice beaches, especially Paradise. As you know, swimming is my biggest fear, but don't worry, I does only go wey the water does reach my knee. I'm in a new school and I have new friends too. Most of the children cool; they not as loud as the ones in GSS. It have a boy that like me; he got me a chair the first day of school and he bought me a chocolate the other day. I like him too. I have a new best friend. Her name is Nicole and she's the principal's niece. But diary, I still feel worthless. Whenever I'm with my friends I pretend to be happy but once I'm by myself I get the urge to cut myself and to commit suicide. I'm not happy and each time I pretend to be, I feel worse about myself. Things at my new home ent too nice either. Mom does make me feel as if I don't belong here and I does be afraid to walk around the house, so I does stay in my room all by myself and that's when everything does run through my mind. I'm feeling as if it was my fault I was raped. I'm really tired of life. I'm tired of everything. I want to go home and meet Jesus. I don't know what else to do. I'm really unhappy. I'll talk to you soon again. Its time for me to go to my bed.

I closed the diary and pushed it back in my going out clothes. I took the bed sheet and wiped the tears running down my cheeks. I shut my eyes close and lay on the bed thinking about everything, wondering if and when things will end. I want to get big fast and have my own job and my own house so that people won't have to cut style on me and treat me as if am nobody.

I have school in the morning so is best I went to sleep. I don't want to be sleeping during class. I does have to catch the bus for seven-thirty.

Chapter 37: Yankee Doodle!

We have a new Information Technology teacher. He just came from

America. He tall and he real muscular. Some of the children say he look like

a giant and when he talk it does sound like when thunder going and roll.

Information Technology is not my favourite subject; I prefer Principles of

Accounts, Principles of Business and Social Studies.

I doh like how that man does teach because he always trying to yank and whenever he start with his foolishness I does find it rather difficult to understand. Me, I just doing Information Technology 'cause they say it's a must.

Sir walked in the class and is like you could hear the ground shake. He too tall for his pants so it cut a little bit above he ankles, and Sir wearing a Clarks—he not wearing a shinny cockroach killer as most of the other male teachers. His plaid shirt tuck in his pants and he nice leather belt showing. Sir swagging and he looking good too. They ent make a special chair for him yet so sometimes he does stand up or force to sit down on one of them small one that he does make look real small. He greeted the class, introduced the topic and we all answered him.

"Today we are going to be looking at bytes."

"We will be looking at what?" I asked because I really doh know what Sir saying. What the ass is bytes in Information Technology.

"Bytes Michelle, bytes." Indira said.

"Sir, you really need to talk for people to understand because that American accent thing ent working good for me nah."

Jeremy poked me on my side.

"Watch what you saying girl," he whispered. Me and Jeremy does share tables. I like sitting next to him because he does make me laugh and even though they say no eating in the class we always eating something.

Sir raise up he head—he head that big like full moon and looked straight at me.

"You saying something Michelle?"

"Yes Sir, I saying ah can't understand you accent; speak normal so I can understand."

Sir looked at me and he start to puff up he face; he doing as if I should never tell him that.

"Then maybe you should check you ears."

"You want to give me permission to go in the clinic and check it Sir?"

Jeremy poke me again and everybody in the class looked at me- some even had their mouths open.

"Michelle I'm not mixing any matters with you eh!"

"Mixing what matters? Sir this is Information Technology not Physics."

Sir look at me and I looked back at him. Sir was angry and I could see that but I ent really care I speaking my mind because if he continue teaching like that I won't understand and that will defeat my purpose of learning and coming to school.

"Get out of my class Michelle. I realise you is one of the students that have no respect and I not in that with you." Sir was talking loud now; he voice echoing in the class. He ent yanking again because I hearing everything he saying clear, clear, clear.

"Get out of you class to go way?" I made myself comfortable on me chair and I leaned back, with me foot crossed on one another and me hand on the side ah the government chair.

"I said get out Michelle, get out or I go put you out!"

I watch Sir sitting down dey, he pants ride up he foot and he socks showing and I know I ent getting up to go no way.

"Sir I ent going no way."

"Well if you ent go, I not teaching no class you in."

"Well nobody just won't learn, because everybody here pay school fees and besides I ent do nothing wrong; all I say is ah can't understand you accent."

Sir got up from the chair and he walked towards my table. Sir big, but me ent fraid ah him. Ah know he can't do me nothing.

"Michelle I said get out!"

Indra got up too—she is the class bully but she real bright (the girl bright like daylight and she does compete with Neila for the first position). Indra thin too—she favor ah grain ah spaghetti.

"Girl you doh hear the man say get out ah the class!" Indra shouting but she voice sounding like a five year old.

"Why you doh come and move me, eh, get out ah which class?"

She walked towards me and Sir told her go back in her seat. The children seemed to be enjoying the commotion.

Same time Miss Quamina walked across the class door, going down the corridor and Sir called out to her. She called me and I walked outside and she asked what the problem is so I explained it to her. You never had to tell her she need to check she ears. She spoke to Sir and then she asked me to follow her to her office.

Chapter 38: My Principal

"Michelle what do you want to be in life?"

I hesitated and looked at Miss Quamina, her long black hair combed in one and she made a doughnut in the end. She was wearing a nice stopper earring and her black skin shining— shining like if she now get polished, just like how the chairs does shine after you sandpaper and polish them for Christmas. Miss Quamina smelt nice, like the perfume store wey me and Nicole does go and sample perfume when school over. Since we don't have money to buy none, we does sample them and go. Sometimes I does wish somebody feel sorry for us and buy us one.

"I want to be a lawyer." I bit my fingernails and looked at the painting with the prime minister on the wall- he big nose spread across his face like butter on hot stone and he grinning. He have nice white teeth and a mole on the left side of his face. People say the prime minister is ah black Syrian because all he doing is selling Grenada. They say he is the reason we have to get visa now to go Canada because he sold our passport for foreigners and they put us on the blacklist.

"And how do you intend to be a lawyer?"

"I will work hard and study, and pass all my exams."

Miss Quamina looked down at me; her face serious. She not even blinking, and her eyes fixed on me. Her eyes boring holes in my skin; it gave me goose bumps and my skin rose. I hate when people stare at me; it does make me feel nervous and I does tremble, the same way how I does tremble when somebody make me afraid.

"Well you need to change your ways Michelle; you can't be fighting and getting on like that, especially being disrespectful to your teachers. You could do well. You have potential but always remember it's not just about academics—you have to walk with your head up and maintain a good reputation."

"But they interfere with me first!"

"It don't matter Michelle. One hand can't clap and every action don't deserve a reaction. Sometimes you have to learn to ignore people. It's better people say you coward."

I kept quiet and I wondered if Miss Quamina know what she was really telling me. How was I to allow somebody to hit me and not hit them back? My mother taught me never to take people lash, because I am not a punching bag.

"Yes Miss Quamina." I said yes but I ent sure if I mean it, because I sure would not walk out the door now and somebody touch me, and I not touching them back.

"Michelle I want the best for you. I know your potential and your teachers speak well of you too. Continue doing well. Just remember to work on your attitude and you will reach far in life. You will be the lawyer you want to be, and one more thing, stop wasting your free time. When you have a free period, take you book and read and prepare for your next class."

"Yes Miss." I bit my fingernail and I stomp my foot in slow motion on the tile flooring—the nice marble tile that clean, clean and pretty.

"Go back to your class and remember all the things I just told you."

I walked out the office breathing a sigh of relief. I passed the receptionist's room wey the secretary always sits down behind the desk and I nodded at her. She smiled at me and I waved my tiny hands, moving them like when dem police does signal them vehicle to stop.

There were some children sitting on the chair below the staircase. I walked pass them and headed to my class. My class is close to the IT room and it's on top the stage wey we does have assembly when rain falling and we can't have it outside.

I saw my best friend Nicole. She was sitting down in she seat and Clara and Jane sitting down beside her.

"Michelle, what Miss Quamina did to you? You get lash?" Nicole asked.

"Nothing," I said, pulling out my chair to sit down beside them.

"Nothing?" Nicole looked surprised and Clara and Jane look surprised too.

"Nothing, she just talked to me."

"What she say?"

"She say I must continue to fight and answer back them teacher and I will graduate with honours."

"Stop lying girl!" We all laughed and I slapped Nicole playfully on her shoulders.

"Allu too fast. You must learn to mind allu dirty business."

We laughed again, then Jane looked at Nicole and said, "Ah have a story for allu."

We all like stories especially when it comes to minding dem popular girls business. I pulled my chair closer because I ent want to miss nothing in what Jane have to say.

"Allu know Debra pregnant?"

"Pregnant?" Me Chubby almost dropped from me hand and I watched Jane in she two cocojay eyes.

"Yes she pregnant and she try to throw the baby, but she bleeding heavy so they have to take her to the hospital."

Nicole opened she eyes, she mouth and she nose and she taking in everything Jane saying. Clara just sit down with her hands under her chin and she looking like them children they does show on TV, that seeing trouble from Africa. It's a big shame to be in school and pregnant; people does talk down on you. It's even worse to try and throw away the baby.I didn't know what to say, so we just look at Jane and we all shake our heads in unison.

Chapter 39: Jeremy

"Michelle!" I pulled the stained blinds that were hanging since Christmas and looked out the window. Jeremy was standing in the road and he looking up at the house bawling out me name as if he christened me.

"What you bawling out me name so for boi? Ah owe you ah wah?"

He laughed. "Girl, come let's go and hunt and see if we get sugar apple."

Ah love star apple and he know that; I love sugar apple more than I love mango and I love mango too eh, but sugar apple sweeter.

"Wait for me, let me change me clothes." I put down the curtain and turned towards the closet (Daddy built the closet with his own hands and he put the door too and he painted it in white). I pulled out a long pants and ah long sleeve jersey. I like going hunting but I don't like when pickers jook me or the grass cut up me skin- it does pain and when it heal it does leave a gallay mark. Mama use to tell me I gallay and I missing one more mark to be a leopard. So I trying hard not to get another mark.

I grabbed my bag and walked to the kitchen for the small knife I does always bring with me when I going in the bush. Ah hear me name again. Jeremy was shouting at me.

"Michelle bring something to eat!"

"Boy leave me alone eh. You pot have hole? Not home you come out?" Jeremy know I only joking so he ent say ah word. I opened the fridge and pulled out a Busta for Jeremy, I walked back in me room and picked up the Rough Top biscuit I had on the sofa. That's all I had so Jeremy had to make that do. I closed the door, took my time and walked down the step because it's not too wholesome. I don't want to fall especially wey Jeremy dey outside waiting- he go laugh at me and I go have to lick him down.

"But Michelle why you have on so much clothes?"

"Boy you feel I want thing bite up me skin?" I pushed the Busta and biscuit at Jeremy. He took it and opened it one time.

"But you doh have nothing to worry about you done gallay ah ready." Jeremy talking and he have a piece ah biscuit in he mouth.

"You must choke. Ah feel to take back me blasted thing from you we. Who you think you calling gallay?"

Jeremy laughed and I laughed too. I watch he Adam's apple grew as he drank the Busta and he throat made a funny noise— like how the dog does sound when it choking.

"Wey we going?"

"For suagr apple girl. We could go and look for an iguana and cook a pot too."

I never liked iguana until I come and live in Carriacou. All wey u go you does see ah iguana—they like leggo beast.

"Oh that sound like a good idea because I hungry. Jeremy you do you homework? What answer you put for number two?"

"Girl what you asking me? Up to now I ent open ah book yet; ah go copy that from you."

"Copy what from who? You think I stupid to do me homework and just give you my answers? Homework is for me alone; you go really have to pay me for it."

"What you want ah kiss?"

"Kiss who? I doh want you dirty mouth on me boy. Kiss my black behind!"

I laughed real loud and Jeremy laughed too—his two front teeth showing.

"Come let me kiss it nah, you feel ah fraid?"

I laughed again, my body shook too.

"Boy you sick you kno, you real sick, you need Jesus!"

We walked through the dirt track. Mango was in season and there was plenty old mangoes on the ground. Sometimes I does come and pick them up for the pig, but not today. I was not in the mood for that and besides, the pig is not mines, so I'm not the one who always have to look for things to feed it. That was the responsibility of the owner.

"Michelle you see that?"

"See what?" Jeremy pointed and I looked wey he was pointing but I ent seeing nothing; all I feeling was the hot sun in me eyes. I blinked but the sun was still burning me.

"Ah ent see nothing."

"Girl you blind, look it have a 'guana dey." Jeremy pointed and this time I saw it—a big 'guana too. It have same color of the leaves that's why I did not see it before. Jeremy dropped the bag he had flung across his shoulder (the bag that look like it doh know the last day it see water; like it and water go in court and water win) and he ran down the little incline. I dropped me bag and ran down the hill too because I want to catch the iguana when Jeremy knock it down. Ah doh want it to get away as the one I made get away the last time we went hunting.

Jeremy was on the tree by the time I reached down and the branch was making noise as if it wanted to break. Jeremy ent care; he climbing still. I under the tree and praying the branch ent break because I don't want Jeremy to fall. Jeremy shok the branch and the iguana fell down 'buff' on the ground. I spun around and I catch it by its tail one time—it was kinda heavy. I held it and knocked it hard on the stone because I don't want it to bite me.

"Michelle you is Bolt? How you catch that fast so?"

"Boy you better get you black ass down from that tree and come and hold you iguana before I let it go and you have to run behind it!"

"Let it go if you bad nah."

I pretend I dropping it and Jeremy flew down the tree.

"Girl you playing mad awah!"

Chapter 40: Cook Up

We lit the fire. I blew until me throat tired because the fire taking its damn

time to catch. We done seasoned the iguana and we have flour so we making

a brown down. When it was time to catch the meat was me and Jeremy alone,

but now that we going and make thing to eat everybody gather.

We does cook right on the side of the road, close to the basketball court, wey my brother always playing with his friends, but nobody ent playing today.

"Blow the darn fire nah girl!"

"Why you doh come and blow it with your horse breath?" Me and Jeremy does always curse but we ent vex with each other. They say Jeremy go be me boyfriend because we does move like husband and wife. But we not on the boyfriend and girlfriend thing; we just good friends. Jeremy does look out for me in school too; he does warn the boys to not come around me and when people interfere with me Jeremy does warn them and tell them leave me alone.

I blow again and the fire catch; some smoke go in me throat and I coughed. I hate when smoke go in me throat—it does make me feel like I choking and water does run down me eyes like if I crying.

"Finally, ah was beginning to think you breath too strong for that fire you know."

"Is not kettle calling pot black; boy you should be the last."

Jeremy ent answer me but Franko laughed. Ah want to ask Franko what he laughing for and wey he was when 'guana catching, but I tired and kinda hungry too. I go ask him later when me belly full. Jeremy take the black iron pot that look like charcoals, and he put it on the three fire stones we put together.

"Frank boy, bring the pot spoon and the sugar for me."

Ah glad he ent ask me because I tired. Franko walked wey Jeremy have he bag with the sugar and he bottom giggle like if he is ah girl. Franko have more bam bam than me; me I ent have bam bam at all. When God was giving bam bam I was in the back ah the line so I ent get none. I flat like ah ironing board, but I don't really care. The bigger the bottom the heavier the weight. I ent want to walk around with no big bam bam. They say people with big bam bam does always have dry mess because they can't wipe it good. So me, I good with me two lime in me socks.

Franko bent down to pick up them things and he Hilfiger boxers showing as if he advertising for the company.

"Franko you feel that looking good? Pull up you pants," Jake said. Jake is my little cousin—Tanty Miranda's son, and he's younger than all of us, but all wey pot cooking he does find it— is like he have dog nose.

Franko took one hand and pulled up he pants and he picked up the pot spoon and sugar with he other hand. He walked back towards us and handed it over to Jeremy.

"Open the plastic for me nah boi, the pot done hot ah ready; let me burn the colouring."

Franko open the plastic bag. He struggled ah little because the plastic bag was tied tight. Jeremy poured some sugar in the pot and the pot made a noise —the same noise it does make when I pour the sugar in the pot to stew me chicken.

I sat down and gazed down the road. The sun was still hot, but it ent hot as it was before. A bus passed and dust blew in me face. I cursed under me breath but nobody ent hear anything. I does curse at anything. If the wind blow too hard I does curse at it too.

I looked at the plum tree that was now flowering and I wish plum was in season. I love plum too and when plum in season I does make plum stew.

"Allu let we play ah game in the meanwhile nah?" Jerrisia said with she voice sounding crack up, crack up.

"What game?"

"Any game."

"Allu let's play catch and boom," Jake said. Everybody turned to watch Jake and I turned to watch him too. What he mean by catch and boom? Who and Jake is company?

"Aye likkle boy, know you damn place eh!" I looked at him and crossed up my eye. Catch and boom is like hide and seek— the only difference is when they catch you they have to boom you. Me, I don't play that game and I don't want to be close to who playing it either."

"Ah joking, ah joking!" Jake said, as he hung his head in shame.

"Let's play cricket instead."

"Yeah cricket is good I have ah ball and ah bat. Jeremy make ah wicket."

I got up and ran home for my bat and wind ball.

"Ah batting first eh, because is my bat and my wicket and I choosing me team first too. Ah pick Jeremy, Franko and Alice. Allu could have the rest."

We played cricket until the pot done cook. I out for a duck but my team won so I celebrating with everybody.

We eat we belly full and we all went to our different homes. I waved at Jeremy and he waved back at me.

"Remember to do your homework dunce head."

"Girl I go take that from you tomorrow."

Jeremy disappeared in the track and I went inside closing the door behind me.

Chapter 41: The Barter System

"Good morning Miss." We all answered in unison.

Mrs Hirnda stood in front of the blackboard with eyes fixed on us. She was wearing a red suit—same material with the one she was wearing the first time I actually saw her. Miss was red skinned and she had bumps on her face that looks like she color is polka dot. She placed her books on the desk and head up the date on the board. I take out me notebook and I head up too.

"Now class, today we will be looking at the barter system. I hope allu completed the homework from yesterday." God alone knows how much I hate homework; I does only do it because I have to. Why people must have work to go home and do? So everything is about school then?

I knew that topic. I done read that in me book that Daddy bought for me, since before she even say read up for home work.

"Anybody know what the barter system is, Kim, Jane, Burke?"

Everybody shook their head.

"No miss I doh know."

I raised up my hands and Miss looked at me. My classmates looked at me too. My hand in the air like when them people raising they hand to beg at the Salvation Army.

"Lets hear what our new classmate has to say then."

"Barter is said to be the exchange of goods without the use of exact definition in the book and I remembered it.

"Very, very good! What's your name again?"

Michelle."

"Class, lets give Michelle a round of applause."

Miss clapped and my classmates clapped too. Nicole watched me and smiled and I stretched out my tongue the same way I does make monkey tricks with my friend.

"And what are some of the characteristics of barter?"

I scratched my head trying to remember because I read that too. I raised my hand again and answered correctly. I even went as far and explaining why money was chosen over the barter system. Miss looked at me and smiled; she seemed so impressed.

The period ended and it was now time for Principles of Accounts. I love Accounts and I always get my books to balance. Some people say Accounts hard but I don't find so. My Accounts teacher loves the ground I walk on. She says she putting her last dollar on me to get an A in CXC, even though CXC is still a year away for me.

●

Chapter 42: Junior Achievers

I was asked by Miss Hamilton, my Principle of Accounts teacher, to join

Junior Achievers, a school entrepreneurship program where you had to come

up with a business idea, as well as have an executive committee to run that

business. It was the very first time I was asked to join any group and I was

very, very excited. Miss assured me that I will do well and it was the best

group for me since I was an excellent business student. So I accepted. On the day of elections I was voted in as the marketing manager, defeating my three

other competitors. At the end, the executive was selected and I was

congratulated together with all my other peers who were selected to be

members of the executive.

After much debate, we finally decided to go into the cake making business and I was given the task of marketing and promoting the business. For the entire day I was super excited. For the very first time in my life I knew what it felt like to be successful, especially against students that were considered to be popular. I just could not wait for school to finish to share the good news with Daddy. My teacher was excited too, she said she had seen great potential in me and that one day I was going to be a successful entrepreneur and business manager.

One thing I liked about going to school in Carriacou is that the bus does drop you off and pick you up right at the school gate, then drop you straight in you yard. It's not like Grenada wey you have to walk to get a bus and when you drop out of the bus you still walking. I knocked the bus as soon as I reach the gap although the driver know exactly wey I going.

"Bye everyone see you tomorrow!" I shouted

I ran up the stairs and straight in the room by Daddy. For the first time in a long time I was feeling happy. Not stressed out and useless like I normally does feel. I pushed the door open and I saw Daddy on his bed. Thank God he was not naked.

"Good evening Daddy," I said, throwing myself on the bed, ruffling the bed sheet that he took time and spread (the pretty bed sheet with the dandelion flowers and the little yellow neck bird). Daddy didn't seem to mind so I dragged my body and made myself comfortable.

"What passing Michelle, like you win the lotto?" Daddy voice was soft—not grumpy like Mr Bowen, my Agriculture teacher. I watched Daddy and laughed. Lotto? How I go win lotto? I don't even have the age to buy ticket much less.

"Daddy ah wish. If I win the lotto now, I leaving school tomorrow."

Daddy looked at me the same way he does look at me when I start to speak negative things. He hates when I'm negative. He does always say what a man speaketh so he shall live.

"You better drop that thought wey you pick it up. If you win lotto you drop out of school? Drop out of which school? You know how important education is eh? You better stop talk crap."

I looked at Daddy and I just laughed with me eyes open big, big and I sounding as if I going to choke. Daddy ent laughing; he serious. He jaw looking hard - hard like the concrete in the road.

"Daddy guess what! Guess what nah."

"Girl if you have something to tell me, tell me nah; I ent good at guessing."

"But Daddy I want you to guess. Ah doh want to tell you just so."

"No Michelle, you go have to tell me." I steupsed in me mind wondering why Daddy so boring. Why he can't make one guess —one guess won't kill him. He just lie down dey looking at me as if what I have to tell him go save he life and he refusing to guess.

"Anyway Daddy, today Miss asked me to join Junior Achievers."

"What is Junior Achievers?" Daddy asked and the same time he made a slap behind a mosquito. He two hands clapped together and made a loud, loud noise.

"Junior Achievers is a program wey you have to come up with a business idea and start a business; it's for all Form Fours in Grenada, Carriacou and Petit Martinique. At the end of the school year, the best business idea and the school that make the most sales will win ah prize."

"Well that's good Michelle, ent you want to be a business person?"

"No, no, I want to be a lawyer Daddy, but I like business. Maybe I will have my own business after I become a lawyer."

"Oh, ok Michelle, if it's a lawyer, I know you will be the best lawyer there is and one day you will defend your father."

"But Daddy, I will have to defend people that get themselves in trouble, so how it is I go have to defend you; you don't get in trouble."

"You never know what tomorrow go bring me daughter, so it's always good to have a lawyer in the family; you never know wey you father go end up tomorrow."

"Daddy that's not all." (I really didn't like wey this lawyer talk going so I changed the topic quick, quick).

"Tell me the rest ah listening." Daddy made another slap again and this time he catch the fella that was putting bite on him.

"Damn nastiness; allu so little but allu talawa."

"It have plenty blood?"

Daddy opened he hand. The mosquito was mashed up fine, fine. The only thing you seeing is the little bit ah blood stain.

"Anyway Daddy, they voted me as the marketing manager, so I'm responsible for all the advertising and promotions and I'm also responsible for collecting information too. The rest ah children vote and I won by a lot. I beat all the rest ah children, even Ben son and he popular, Daddy."

"Michelle I tired tell you, achievements is not about popularity."

"Yes Daddy, it's about who you know and who know you."

Daddy watched me another bad eye and I knew one time is because I going down the wrong track.

"Listen Michelle, achievement is based on meritocracy—what you work for is what you get. The children voted for you because they know you can do a good job; they voted for you because they know your potential and having you there will be a good representation."

I shook my head in agreement.

"But Daddy, you think I go do a good job, you think I will be a good marketing manager?"

"That will be up to you Michelle. What I know is once you put your mind to something and you put your best foot forward it will be achieved. You have to believe in yourself; don't just let people believe in you. Be confident and as I does always tell you, remain positive."

"But Daddy I positive."

"You think so? If you was positive you would not ask me that question."

I ease myself up the bed because I don't really have time for the lecture.

"Daddy what you cook? I hungry."

"Go in the kitchen and you go see."

I heave off the bed, tapped Daddy on his foot (he foot hairy, hairy like if he is ah spider. Ah doh know why he ent shave them hair. I does wonder how Mom does take that hair on she body). I burst through the door and dive straight to the kitchen with me bag still on me back and ah ent even change my clothes.

"Michelle!"

"Yes daddy?"

"Doh eat all the meat eh, because nobody else ent eat yet."

"Ok ah hear you."

I opened the pot on the stove and me belly rumbled like when thunder rolls. Steam rose as soon as I take out the pot cover and the sweet tasty aroma of pelau filled the air. Yummy! I smiled to myself as I reached for the plate remembering Daddy said not to eat all the meat. Hmmm, I was going and full me belly. I fill the bowl, put down me bag and sit down on the sofa.

Pixie the cat came and pushed she self right below me with she white fur rubbing against me school socks. If Pixie only know how I hate cats, she ent coming close to me. She started making some stupid noise that I can't take. So, I just take piece ah meat and throw it down on the ground. The meat ent reach the ground yet but the greedy cat down catch it ah ready. She moving as if that piece of meat is the meat that go save she life and she ent eat for days.

"Meow, meow, meow." I raised me foot and I just kicked Pixie in the corner. She made a loud, loud noise as if she want to beat me. The same time Daddy called from the room

"What you doing the cat Michelle?"

"Nothing, nothing Daddy. She just greedy so she making noise."

Pixie looked at me as if to tell me: *hush you lying mouth.* I swear if she was closer to me, this time I was kicking her outside.

•

Chapter 43: Preparing For Exams

I eat me belly full, as if I ent get food for days, belched and put me dirty

wares in the sink. I ent have no time to wash dishes; somebody else go wash

it when they come home or Daddy go wash it if he see it in the sink for too

long. Daddy hates nastiness. He does always say cleanliness is next to

godliness and nastiness is not a good trait. But me, I lazy as a church rat; it's

not easy to just sit down on a bench for all these hours. Plus everyday is ah set ah home work and end of term exams is just around the corner so I have

to study because I want to pass everything and get good grades too.

I already know what it feels like to fail, so I want to know how it feels to pass and do well. So far am doing well in class. Most of my exams I does get more than eighty five percent. Sometimes I does even get better grades than Sara—the girl that accustom coming first. Her friends does tell her she get competition and she does vex. She does stretch she mouth long like Point Salines airport and she lip done over hanging ah ready so it does never be a pretty sight.

I'm not competing with anybody. I just want to make a change and do well so that I can be independent and break the cycle of poverty so that nobody won't have the cause to abuse me again. I want better for myself and I want to make good use of Daddy's money. I don't want it to go down the drain because he trying to make sure I have all that I need for school. I have to make him proud, I have to raise he nose and make him see he ent spending he money in vain.

The people that say I would drop out of school—I want to prove them wrong, especially Mama. Although she said I won't reach in Form Three but now I'm in Form Four. I want them to see that I am better and stronger than what they say I will turn out to be, and they bad mouth ent breaking me; it just making me stronger. I want to be able to get a good job when I finish school. I want to go to college too but I must pass more than five subjects.

Daddy said if I want to excel, I must study hard and pay attention when my teachers are teaching. Daddy does always warn me about bad company. He say friends does bring you go, but they don't always bring you back, and life ent running and leave me, so I must pay attention to the things that are important for now, until the time for other things come along. I know what Daddy means very well. He means I must put my books before boys. But I don't really have much boys to study. I just want better for myself.

When I slacking he does punish me. He don't beat me or curse me like Mama, but his punishment worse than Mama own and sometimes I does wish he just beat me and done because it will pain for a few minutes and then I'll be normal again.

Daddy does take away all the things I like, and if he know I want to go somewhere and I do something bad he ent making me go, so I does always have to be on me Ps and Qs and make sure my grades, behaviour and everything else in order too. Daddy does not even miss one of my PTA's. Once he on the island he coming and if he ever get one bad complaint is discipline in me backside. He has a good relationship with my teachers too so that does keep me from slipping up because I don't like testing Daddy's fate and worse of all, I don't like enduring these punishments. Sometimes when I do behave bad for the whole weekend, I can't go on the computer. I can't even check me Hi5 profile or talk to my friends on MSN. He does take away my phone too and I does have to stay inside that boring house where I can't even put on the TV because its part of my punishment too.

I does just lock the door and stay inside me room. I don't even talk to nobody on them days because I does feel ah kinda hatred for Daddy even though I know what he doing is just to get the best for me. Daddy say I rebellious and I have to change my ways, because sometimes when he talk I does give him back answer. I does steups too without even knowing I steupsing because it's just a bad habit that I trying to break out—ah bad habit that always gets me in trouble. To steups is just another way of saying: *kiss me black Grenadian ass*, and that's very disrespectful.

I opened me room door and as usual, things laying everywhere. Ah see me IT book in the corner on the floor and the clothes I wore yesterday by my bed head. Whenever Daddy come in my room we does fall out. He say as a young lady I have to keep my space better than that, but the more I tidy up, the things always find they self scatterred about again. So sometimes I does just leave them and don't bother waste my time. I picked up the dirty clothes and throw it in me dirty clothes basket and picked up the book from the ground too. This is a new book but it done have dog ears ah ready and one of the page looking as if it ready to come out.

I removed my tie and opened the window. Cobweb tie up me hand as if is thread and the window looking like it ent know the last day it clean. I raised up the blinds and made a knot so that breeze could come in, then I took out the rest ah uniform and changed my clothes.

I opened my bag and it made the same old noise that does always annoy me. Ah never see a bag so big and with so much pockets. The bag could hold my books plus all the other books of my classmates, fuss it big and ugly. It look like Scary Movie 3. I does have to make up me mind whenever I going in it.

I pulled out my exam time table and looked at my exams schedule. My first two end of term exams were Agriculture Science and Social Studies. It was going to be better if I study Agriculture Science because Social Studies is ah common sense subject. I don't have to study plenty for that, but Agriculture Science is ah set ah drawing and labelling and ah can't even draw for me plate ah food. I took out the Agriculture Science book. It green and have some students on it; not Grenadian students—they look like they from Guyana or Barbados because they shirt not in their skirt—it's overlapping. We don't wear our uniforms like that. Our shirts does have to be tucked in our skirt or pants. They standing under a tent with crops and each of them have notepads in their hands. I looked at the cover for almost five minutes trying hard to figure out what country it was before I actually opened the book and start to study.

The exam was going to come on germination and the types of soil as well as plant rotation. I knew most of the definition but the complicated part for me was the drawing and labelling, especially when it came to drawing the seed. The seed looked so easy to draw but it hard and I does always get mixed up with the cotyledon and the micropyle. Don't matter how much I draw and label, I always getting it mixed up. When it comes to that, me head hard as rock stone because I just can't get it right. I drew and drew until I finally get it right. I went over the definitions, writing them down on me study exercise and then I closed my book.

I peeped outside and to my surprise it was getting dark ah ready. L'Esttere is really a quiet place sometimes. The only noise you does hear is when them hungry mongrel dogs barking or them neighbours shouting out to call one of their children, especially cousin Joyce.

"Ron, Ron pass you ass here. Ron you duh hear ah calling you? Wey the ass you dey?" Cousin Joyce always calling Ron and as soon as he returns, before long he disappears and she calling again, disturbing the peace of the neighbourhood. Me, I done get accustom to her already so when I hear she pumping up, I does just repeat what she going and say in my mind. Poor Ron, he giving the woman headache. Ah doh know why he can't just stay at his home.

Chapter 44: Basket Mouth Nicole

I got up early and took a bath. The cold water hit me skin and I got goose

bumps. I took the soap, rub it on me panty and I rub it hard below me arm so

that all the sweat will wash off and nobody won't have the cause to tell me

my perspiration stink. I rub me back, then me belly and I throw some water

on my skin to rinse out the soap that foamed on my body just like how it does

foam in the bucket when I washing my dirty clothes on a weekend. I bent down over the bucket and washed up and when the water touch me thing it

ent burn as how it use too; down they heal now and nobody don't force they

way inside me anymore. I got up from over the bucket and raised it up and

splash the remaining water on me skin. I grabbed the towel from the wall,

wrapped it around me skin and walk out the bathroom.

"Good morning Mom." Mom was walking towards the bathroom with her soap in her hand.

"Morning." Ah know she answering me just because Daddy dey. I know she don't really have nothing much to say to me either. Mama does move just so when Uncle Jack children use to come to spend weekends; she always walking with she face puffed up and not answering them when they talking. I ent no fool. I accustom to that kind of behaviour and I know Mom ent really want me in she place. If it was up to her, I would not have been there in the first place.

I walk through my room door pushing it and turning the knob behind me.

My biggest fear is for someone to see my nakedness, hence I does always lock the door. I dried my skin making sure all the water came out before I greased myself down with the Vaseline—the one that Daddy brought from he trip in Tortola. I doh put plenty because I ent want me skin to start shining and for people to ask me if I fall down in oil. I put the roll on below my arm and it made me skin raise again because it cold and sticky. I put on me rest ah clothes, told Daddy bye, collected the money he had for me and ran out the house.

I walked down the road and saw blinds raising as if people have something outside looking for. Me eyes made four corners with Miss Jack. She pulled back she head fast—ah never know ah old woman had so much speed in she head.

I smelled the bread, mixed with cinnamon, and the currants roll and my belly rolled as if I ent eat for days. I really don't know wey I get that greediness from, but I just passed the bakery straight and walked down to the bus stand.

The paint on the bus stop was peeling off and nobody was seeing the need to repaint it. Piece ah galvanise looked like any minute it go fly away too but nobody ent really care. I crossed the road with me two legs rubbing and I bumping as if me is ah little boy.

"Good morning everybody." Ah keep me head high and I stood in the far corner of the bus stand. Ah know anytime from now the bus was going to come.

"Good morning, good morning." Everyone answered in unison.

Peep, peep, peep. I knew that sound. I din have to wait for the bus to break the corner to see is Putty. I waited until the bus stopped and I jumped inside. Me heart beating fast, fast in me chest because the time for exams drawing closer and I hoping the questions they bring is the questions I study for because I have to pass and I have to get an A too. Shit make if they bring something else.

"Nicole gyal you study?" I saw Nicole as I burst the gate. She was just standing there grinning at me, grinning as if she is ah stupidee and she big teeth in front she mouth showing.

"Study, gyal study what, you know how tired I was last night?"

I just watched Nicole and shake me head.

"You study?"

"Girl yes, I read up on germination and the different types of soils and I practiced how to draw and label the seed. Ah only hope what I study for will come."

"Oh, well germination ent a hard topic; man I should be fine, but honestly girl, I can't take the study thing."

I turned up me eyes the same way I does turn it up when something go in it.

"And how you expect to pass your exams?"

"Doh worry about me ah safe; ah must pass."

"Let's go in the school compound you hear. If you say you safe, you safe."

I looked across the road and in front the shop full ah school children. Ah wondering in me mind if they ready for they exam because most of them does be busy to ask for answers and when you don't give them, they does want to be vex more than you. Me and Nicole walked through the gate and we greeted the security. She just smiled at us and I smile back (she in the little kennel they build in front the gate they call a security booth). Ah sure if I bring me dog dey she running away.

I walked and sat down on the wall bench (the children in the construction class built it for their practical). The edges of the bench were rough as some of them face and the backrest dab up with paint like when you give a child a colouring book and crayon to colour.

"Michelle what you thinking about?"

"Nothing gyal."

"Nothing me big foot. You feel I ent know you, you thinking about something."

I sucked my teeth again.

"Well since you know me more than I know me self tell me what I thinking about nah."

"You thinking about Hunter."

Ah get up quick, quick and I put me hand over Nicole mouth. I looked around to make sure no one was listening and my heart started to race like ah engine. What the ass was really taking this blasted girl!

Nicole giggled but I darn serious. Why the ass she had to mention the boy name. Yes I love him bad, more than pig loves mud and bees love honey, but that's not everybody's business.

"Hush you blasted mouth!"

"But Michelle,"

"Michelle me caca. Don't practice you foolishness!"

"But you like him ent?"

"And so?" I put me hands on me hips and turn up me eyes, winking up me eyelids as if pepper fall in my eyes.

"You must be proud of what you have."

"Proud of what I have? You find I know how to make man? The people man ent mines. I just like him."

"But he like you too."

"And how you know that?"

"Because I see the way he looking at you, grinning as if he is ah monkey. He eyes does be boring holes in you uniform. You think I does not watch him eh. And I does watch you blushing too as if you win a ticket to the Bahamas. Hmm, you telling me about allu."

I looked at Nicole and my heart beating in fast and slow motion. Just he name alone sweeping me off my feet; just the simple thought of him—his big shoulders and muscular body. The boy fine, fine, fine and he have some big, big, pretty eyes—eyes that look like a marble. I like him not for sex or anything. I just like him bad bad bad.

"Nicole ah hear you. Let's not talk about people and start talking about we self and the exam we have coming up, because you see me, I don't want to fail."

"Fail? Michelle you and I know we not failing anything, especially you—not with that big brain you have they. Failure can never be a word in your book."

"Big brain or not let us revise the people work eh. Ah sure the person name you mention done study ah ready."

I sat back down on the pattern of a bench and Nicole sat down too. We revised till the bell rang. I asked Nicole questions and she answered and whatever she got wrong I asked her over and over again until she answered it correctly.

Chapter 45: Overwhelmed

Thank God everything I had studied for came in my end of term exams. The

exams were real easy. No hard set of questions. I wrote until I was tired and

everytime I glanced at Nicole she was writing too. So I know it must have

been easy for her as well. The only exam I found to be difficult was Maths—

ah set ah thing the darn red man ent even teach.

However, at the end of the term, my average was 81.9. I was happy. I felt proud and excited. I was making progress; my grades and performance in school were improving and my teachers and friends appreciated me. I was no longer the dunce bat failing all my exams and going in school just to hear the bell ring. I was taking things seriously and the results were evidence of my hard work and determination. I felt the change and I smiled—gosh I was enjoying that moment. Daddy said there was still room for improvement and if I pay a little more attention to school, I was going to do better. Daddy does always push me to be better. He says he wants the best for me and I believe him because even if he does hardly be home, he always provides my school needs.

In GSS my average used to be all kind of 13.3 so to move to such a high average that's a rather big accomplishment. My teachers liked me and sometimes I does go in the office on my break time and spend time with them. I does borrow some of their books and go home and read. CXC is only one year away and I want to do well. Some children does say I feel I bright and I does play I know it all, but that's not really the case. I does spend plenty time in my books and I does write down things over and over so that I will understand.

The boy who liked me and I had liked him ent like me again. He said he still do but he has another girlfriend and she's in my class. I had grown attached to him so everytime I see him with the other girl I does get real jealous and upset. Sometimes I does cry too, because my heart not feeling glad as it use to; it's broken now and he makes me feel bad.

But there is another boy I like too—ah doh really like him— well another boy that does trouble me. He say we should have a relationship, but he's much older than I am and he is working; he not going to school. He not as handsome as Hunter. He head big and he short with some teeth pointing in all kind of direction. Sometimes I does hear Daddy and them talking about him. They say he's a rather disrespectful person and that he is somebody young girls should stay away from.

I prayed silently in my heart thanking God for his goodness and mercies and for blessing me with wisdom, knowledge and understanding. I had the strength to work hard and change my grades, to pass my exams and surpass all my expectations. The feeling was sweet, sweet as the taste of condensed milk on my tongue or maybe even sweeter. I was not dunce after all. Maybe it was just a matter of applying myself and being comfortable, having people to push and encourage me instead of wishing me all the bad things life had to offer. I was rather thankful; it was really better late than never. All I had to do now was continue to study and to apply myself, so that I can maintain my good grades and if possible, graduate with honours and win a scholarship. I know it was going to take a lot to happen and all I had was just one year to accomplish that. It was going to be a series of hard work, late nights and plenty studying, but if that's what it was going to take, I was prepared and ready—ready to make all the necessary sacrifices to be a better person and to achieve my goals and make a difference not just for myself but my family. The past was already gone all I had control over was the future.

Daddy was happy about my grades but some how Mom was not pleased. She was giving me the cold shoulders again when I told her of my accomplishments. But I was not going to allow her to steal my joy. I was happy for myself. To hell with her if she was not happy for me.

Chapter 46: Things At Home

School ent going too bad, but things changed at home. Daddy does spend

plenty time on the sea and Mom does move like she don't really like me.

Sometimes she does cook and not give me food and she does tell me come

out of she house and go. When Daddy calls I don't tell him anything because

I don't want to create problems for the people. I came and met them happy so

I leaving it like that. I does try to avoid her once I'm home. I spend lots of time with my friends—my boyfriends of course. I kinda rather having boys as

my friends. Other than not liking confusions as girls, they does teach me new

things.

Jeremy is my best male friend. He living at the top of the hill, right in the shortcut wey you have to pass to go on Paradise beach. Jeremy has other brothers and sisters and sometimes I does play with them too. I can catch fish and climb coconut trees. Jeremy and them can't climb so I'm the one to drag up the tree when we feeling for jelly. Some people say I'm a tomboy and that I move like one since I always on some tree and I'm always fighting. It's not that I always fighting, but when people hit me. I just hit them back because I'm not allowing anybody to take advantage of me, not after all that I went through. So anybody that want fight, does get fight. I don't care how big you are or how strong you are either, once you hit me that is it. I will be hitting back and I fighting with my last breath if I have to. Them children in my class don't take chances with me either.

There was this boy from school that I liked. It feels so good liking someone. My heart does feel like it growing in me chest and I does get butterflies in my stomach and little worms tickling me head. But I ent brave as the other girls who does be kissing all over the place. I can't bring myself to kiss in public. I don't even know how to kiss. But I know that I like him and he say that he likes me too. Sometimes I help him with his school work and he helps me with any drawing I have to make.

One day for my birthday I asked Daddy to go to a dance show on the tennis court. The tennis court is a big place where most of the activities take place, and its right behind the police station. Whenever they have something there, the music is really loud and Carriacou people loud and wild—they does make more noise than the music and I does wonder how them police does get to sleep and cope with the noise. But the police does be on the court enjoying themselves too.

Anyway I got permission and I went. I put on me nice skinny jeans and me top and sandals my cousin gave me before she went back to America. I lifted the mattress from my bed and took $35 out of my savings.

When I arrived I saw my big brother with his friends.

"What you doing here Michelle?" I could smell the rum on his breath. The show ent start yet and the boy drunk ah ready with his friends.

"Ah liming you can't see?" Ah answered with an attitude on me face.

He looked at me and he could hardly stand. He swaying like a tree that trying to decide if it should stand or fall.

"Time to go home girl, go home."

Go wey? Who that boy think he was talking to? Is like he see his friends and he want to show off. He know how I reach in town?

"You know how I come here eh?" I asked with my hands on my waist and I looking up at him.

"I don't know how you come, but I telling you go home."

"Ah ent going no way and if you want me to go, jump in you car and come and drop me; it's my birthday plus its my money and I got permission."

"You playing you forward!" With that the boy just box me across me face. I started cursing. Ah told him if he want child to hit he should go and make, because he have no right to hit me. I was going to hit him back but when I pushed him I realise my strength was nothing compared to his.

"Watch how I go mash up you fricking car and burn all you clothes! Because you dey around you friends you trying to play dottish? You is me freaking father? You know how I grow to reach this age?"

We were both exchanging words. Looking around I saw a nail, picked it up and walk towards his car. I was going and puncture each and every tyre.

Luckily a policeman came to settle the dispute. I had no desire to stay in the show again so I decided to just go home. All that was on my mind was to burn all his clothes.

Chapter 47: Get Out!

I woke up the next morning still mad as ever, because I really can't

understand for a big man why my brother had to be an ass and show it.

There was a knock at my room door and I let go a big steups.

"Who is it?" I asked.

"It's me." I heard my sister's voice muffling with the fan breeze.

"Hold on." I jumped out from under the cover. All I have on was me bloomers. I don't like sleeping with much clothes, even though I have the fan turned on, I does still feel hot—is like I have an extra heat. I turned the knob and the door made a noise as if the knob rusty and it need some WD40.

"Dale, what is it?"

"You have a text message on you phone." I stopped breathing for a while fighting to not inhale the pee scent coming from Dale. Big girl like her still peeing bed as if she is ah infant! I had left the phone to charge in the living room, because for whatever reason the outlet in my room was not working.

"Give me the phone." She passed the phone and I closed the door. The scent making me want to sneeze, but I ent have nothing to tell the people children because I ent have luck.

I opened the text and I read the message and immediately

I started to shake: *Don't let me come back and see you in my house. Pack all you belongings and go.*

I really didn't know what to think. Daddy only recently came back for the weekend. What in God earth could have made Daddy ask me to leave his place? My brother must have told him another version of what actually happened. But why Daddy never asked me a question, why he ask me to leave his place and to make it worse is text he text me? He ent even have the audacity to ask me a question. If is one thing I don't like is people telling me go from their place. I hate to be in people place and don't feel welcome. And my sister know what the text say because she done read it ah ready. I got up from my bed, (seriously I was not in any mood to make it up so I just throw my cover on the pillow) and walked out the room. My room close to the veranda and it's where Daddy and Mom have their bedroom, I walked outside and the board made a creeky sound (it's a piece of board that need changing).

I knocked on Daddy's door, but no one answered. I really wanted to find out from him why he have to ask me to leave his place and go, and what I did to deserve this text. If he knew he never wanted me, why did he take me out of the people home and bring me wey he and he wife and children ent like me.

I was really upset and I didn't know how to mask it. I was feeling to curse God too. I wanted to know why He was putting me through all that. Why my suffering can't end? And more I pray to dead is more I remained alive. Now that Daddy asked me to leave where am I suppose to go? Who am I suppose to go by? I don't know wey to go and who to go by, but for sure am going. I called Daddy phone too and he take long, long before he could answer. When he did answer he said, "Just leave me place don't let me come back and see you."

Daddy never accustom behaving so; something had to be terribly wrong for him to be telling me that. But if he say go, I have to go—that's not my place and I don't know how it build.

My only option was to go back Grenada; so my only choice was to contact Mama. Not that I really wanted to go in she place, but lately Mama does call me on me cell phone—the Nokia phone me brother buy for me. This is the phone I does write poems on and play games with.

Mama tell me I must come back home and I must write a letter saying I lied on Uncle Jack so that he could come back home. Mama also told me that if I don't write the letter, they go work obeah on me and I won't know any peace.

Uncle Jack's sister does call too; she say she go pay me if I write the letter; she say when I finish write the letter I should go by a JP and sign it and send it down to Grenada.

I does only listen to them. I not doing that because I ent lying on Uncle Jack. He use to boom me so why they want me to write a letter for him to come out of prison? If he so wanted to come out why he never beg the police to send him home, the same way he beg the doctor to send him home the last time he was in the hospital? Mama say he is ah big dottish man and she wish he did dead.

Once they make me end up in the hospital too. I tried telling Mama that Uncle Jack was booming me and they both gave me ah beating of my life. When they were finished, blood was coming out from me nose and me mouth. Thank God for the neighbour because if it was not for her Mama and Jack would have killed me.

So I dialed Mama's number and told her what happened. Mama seemed all excited. She told me to buy a ticket and come back down and she go send somebody on the boat to meet me and she go get me back in GSS. Mama was being rather nice and I was really surprised.

I got back inside and packed my stuff, put me shoes in one bag and my clothes in another. I spent the rest of the day crying and wondering why I have to be going through all that; why my cross has to be so heavy. I don't really want to go back to Grenada but I ent have a choice because the man ent want me in his place and what hurting me the most, up to now I ent know what I did for Daddy to tell me that.

Chapter 48: Come Down From The Boat

Osprey is a real nice boat; it ent old and rusty as Amelia and it ent slow

either. Osprey does take one hour to reach in Grenada. But them big old boat

does take forever—all kind of 4 hours you does have to be on the sea and the

boat always rocking as if it want to fall down.

"Stacy I going back Grenada." I told my cousin when I reached the junction with me bag on me back and I pulling the suitcase. Stacy is ah nice girl and I like her. She in Form Five and when I have homework I does go by her and she does explain everything to me until I understand. She is my role model, but I does not tell her that. I does really look up to her because she bright and she does take her work seriously.

"Michelle why you going?" Stacy asked with she head peeping out the door in the veranda.

"Daddy say go, so I not staying in his place."

"Girl go back home, you father maybe joking."

"No ah ent going back; ah going in Grenada."

Stacy shook her head and I told her bye-bye. I went under the shade and put down me bag waiting for a bus to pass. It was already 3:00pm and the boat was leaving 3:30 pm. A bus finally came and I jumped inside. The distance from L'Esterre to Hillsborough ent too long so I ent have nothing much to worry about.

Town always boring, don't matter the day. That's the only town I see that never have people. It could never be like Grenville or Gouyave. Don't matter how late you walk the road in Gouyave you must see people. Dey say Gouyave people don't sleep. But Hillsborough dead, dead; not even dogs you can see walking. The only time you seeing people is when it have some kind ah festival.

I dropped out the bus and walked towards the jetty, turned round and saw my police friend and waved to him. He waved back at me and I smiled.I walked through the old red gate. It had plenty other people on the jetty waiting to go on the boat too. I glanced at the water where my friend and I does sometimes bathe. I can't swim so I does mostly stay on the shore or swing on the tire. I walked up to the lady that sells tickets and gave her my name and eighty dollars. She wrote my name on a book, pulled out a pink paper and hand it over to me. I took it from her and stuck it in my pocket. I like to tuck things in my pocket. I had some money and two mints tucked in my pocket too. The ticket made a sound as it touch the rest ah paper.

Sun not too hot so I stood on the jetty and enjoyed the scenery of Carriacou, I looked up in the hills at the hospital, I looked at the rocks how they formed pretty and I was taking in everything. I doh know when I go see Carriacou again.

The boat blew its horn. It was time for people to get inside the boat. I looked at the wristwatch on my hand and it said 3:25. In five minutes I was going to be on my way to Grenada. I jumped from the jetty and reached straight inside the boat. One ah the worker tried to assist me but I tell him no. I have long legs so jumping for me is easy.

At 3:35 the boat was still docked. I watched outside and I saw two police. I spotted Daddy too. He was talking to the captain - no wonder the boat ent leave.Daddy spotted me and he forgot the captain and walked closer to the boat.

"Come down from that boat Michelle." I looked at him with anger in me eyes and anger all over me face. Come down from which boat?

"Ah not coming down from any boat. You told me to come out ah you house. I'm not staying wey I not welcome."

Daddy look defeated; he tapping his hand on he foot.

"Michelle I said come down!" People gathered around now because everybody want to go and they hear me shouting at Daddy. Daddy talked to the policeman and he jump on the boat.

"You ent hear you father say come down?" I watched the policeman and gripped the iron rod on the boat tight, tight. The police was about to move me, but then he remembered as a male he not suppose to touch me.

"Go and call Sam," he said to the next officer, "Tell her come here now."

I know Sam. She is a rough police and she does not make joke, but me I ent care. Daddy say go so I going. Ah doh know what right he have to come and pappyshow himself here now. Like he forget he ask me to go? And when I go he telling me to come? What, he feel I am a dog?

Sam came and she jumped on the boat and I ran towards the bow. I was going and jump in the water. I know it deep and ah can't swim but I doh care; ah was going and kill myself. Ah was tired with everybody and ah was tired with everything. Sam ran after me and grabedb me just as I was about to jump off the bow.

"Michelle you young and stupid, ah go show you who old and dottish!" She pulled at my pants and tugged back. People were making noise and quarrelling with the captain because they all wanted to go.

I tugged and tugged and finally Sam got me on the jetty. I was bawling and I making real noise ah cursing Daddy too.

"Hush you mouth!" Sam said.

"Me damn mouth is mines you can't tell me that!"

Sam raised she hands and box me. I pulled back me hand and I box her too.

"I am not your companion," she said.

"You is not me mother," I replied.

She dragged me to the police station and I stuck me fingers down in her flesh, squezzing hard. I looked back and I could see Daddy following. I gave him one bad eye and turned my eyes in front. It was the first time In my life I felt so much hatred for Daddy.

Chapter 49: Inside The Police Station

"What seem to be wrong with this child?" Sam asked Daddy. Daddy was sitting on the chair with his back leaning, facing the Regatta Jupa, the white hair poking out on his face, indicating it was time for Daddy to shave. He was not looking at me, but he looking at Sam. I was sitting in the corner on a bench quite furious—if ah fly rush me ah killing it.

"Lately ah really doh know what happened to Michelle. Last night me big son told me he tried to talk to Michelle, and it ent have what Michelle ent tell him."

"Why you doh ask ah question before you run you damn mouth," I hissed with anger.

"Michelle is your father you talking to in that manner?"

"It could have been Jesus; I doh care!"

I really did not care. The fact that Daddy had asked me to leave his place only meant that he was my enemy and he was added to my hate list. What had me even more upset was the commotion he created. He asked me to leave and when I left, he made it look as if I ran away from his home, and them stupid police worse than him because they came and take me from the boat.

"Have respect before I put you in the cell!" Sam shouted.

I sucked my teeth and looked at Sam. Her police uniform looking as if it want to choke her. She ugly like thing that ent good; she face looked like them thing on Sesame Street.

"Cell was made for human beings. You feel I fraid you and the cell? Put me dey nah." I sucked my teeth again and Daddy looked at me. He face was looking as if he vex, but I didn't care.

Same time me cell phone rang and I answered. I had called my friend and told him to come and meet me on the boat so I guess he was calling to find out if I left. Before I could say hi, Madam Sam barked at me and told me to put down me phone. Like she is the one that buy phone for me or she is the one that does put credit? I was sitting in the police station and I ent even afraid. I ent care bout the police and ah ent even care about Daddy. Not anymore.

"Who is it calling you?"

"None of your business."

"Michelle, you need to know your place and have some respect for the officer."

"Daddy, ah mean Mr Man, please don't tell me anything." I pulled the chair further and turned my back. I knew deep down Daddy wanted to get up and cut me ass but he just sitting there staring at the wall as if is the first time he see a wall in his life.

"This child is very rude and she needs to be disciplined; look how she talking to you. If was my child all now so I cutting she ass."

Like she never know is rudeness that make me? Cut who ass? If Daddy did only hit me I was going to hit him back.

"I know how to deal with Michelle," Daddy said, he still looking at the wall.

Know how to deal with me? I wish Daddy would just hush he mouth and go about he business; he know how to deal with what. If he really knew how to deal with me, why did he ask me to leave his place and pretend now that he care so much? My brother's side of the story was worth listening to, but what I had to say was not anybody's concern.

They talked for almost an hour and then finally the police van dropped us home. I kept quiet all the way down thinking about what I could have done to get back at Daddy and his children and them that ent like me.

Chapter 50: More Drama

I reached back inside the house and slammed the door behind me. It made a

loud noise and the whole house shook. Mom was sitting on the chair with her

feet folded one on top the other. I just passed her straight without even saying

goodnight and ignored her frozen eyes on my body.

I knocked my fist in the bed and tears flooded down my cheeks again. I felt broken and useless. At that very moment all I felt in my heart was hatred, not just for Daddy but for everything and everyone around me.

I could hear Daddy's voice in the living room talking to Mom assuring her that he will take care of everything. I had the urge to just go outside take a knife and just stab up the whole ah freaking them and let police come for me and let me go and sit down in Richmond Hill.

I felt tired, tired of life, tired of the struggles, the heartaches, the constant reminder that I was a nobody and a floor mat and people was just going to continue treating me anyhow - anyhow as if I ent have owner and I just begging a lodging. I was finding it even more painful trying to figure out the cause of Daddy's sudden behaviour. The same Daddy that used to encourage and motivate me, I was trying to understand why all of a sudden he ent want me in his place and asking me to go, knowing fully well

I have nowhere to go. I couldn't seem to find any answers and that in itself was making me even angrier.

"Michelle!" Daddy called me from the living room.

"Doh call me blasted name!" I shouted.

"You see the same thing I telling you, this little girl have no respect, I ent know what you still have her here doing." It was Mom's voice. Ah ent even let she words drop; it ent reach the ground yet and I pick her up ah ready—to hell with what Daddy thought of me—I ent care about a blasted thing anymore.

"Ah ask allu to be in allu stinking place? Why you husband never leave me on the boat when I was going? The only reason allu getting on like that is because I in allu stinking place, and you this woman, you better not fret me eh. Just let me have some respect for you!" I was shouting, screaming and cursing at the top of my voice and L'Esterre is ah quiet place, so the neighbours listening because they faster than Usain Bolt—everybody's business they minding but they can't see what going on under they own roof.

"Michelle, shut you mouth and don't get me angry!" Daddy snapped. He voice serious but he ent loud; he ent making noise and he echoing across the partition.

"Hush which mouth? You think you paying rent for me mouth? Why you ent tell you wife hush she mouth?"

"Michelle don't let me have the cause to break down that door eh!"

"Break it down! Is you money that spend for it; you think is mines?"

"Daddy, is not you and Mom Michelle speaking to so?" It was Chris—my brother. I knew it was him the minute his foot made the loud noise on the step.

"Who else? Michelle ent know she place you know; is quite down the road I stay and hear her. What she come making she noise here for, and to make it worse she disrespecting?"

"Big bad wolf now that you come, what you go do about it eh, you go beat me the same way you good for nothing brother beat he big daughter? Anyone of allu just play bad and open that room door. Matter of fact, I coming outside. Raise allu hand and hit me and see if I ent burning down this fricking house with all of allu in it. Allu think I is ah wash pan? Raise allu hand and hit me nah, ah ent fraid allu you know!"

I opened the door with the same strength I used to close it and it made a loud noise again, causing the little cupboard with the books to crumble to the ground with books scattering every where.

Chris was standing close to Daddy; his red handkerchief tied around he neck because kill him dead he is ah bloods and he is a bad man. He looked at me and I could see the anger on his face.

"Do what you have to do nah, you come talking as if somebody fraid ah you. Ah tell you ah fraid ah anybody. The fact that I begging a lodging here making allu think allu could treat me and do me what allu want. Not me you kno, not freaking me!"

Chris walked towards me and I felt the sting on my face as his hands connected with my jaw bone. I leaped longer and higher than I does leap for high jump.

"Chris, don't put yourself in trouble for this stupid little girl!" his mother said.

"Stupid? Why you doh bend down and look up you go see stupid!"

My hands connect on his T-shirt. I tugged and pushed, fighting hard to grab his chain, to pull it and break it into pieces. He saw my hands grabbing for his throat and pushed me. I balanced on my feet and launched another attack. I smiled from within as my hands felt the coldness of the gold and I pulled with all my might.

"So you bust me chain eh?" He sounding as if he catching short breath and I standing there feeling satisfied. Daddy ent talking much but I could feel his eyes on me.

"Doh touch me again you kno, cuz I go stab you up. I ent joking eh."

I pushed him and ran out the house. He ran out in the veranda and Mom and Daddy ran out too.

I flew down the stairs. Outside was dark as coal dust and the light from the pole straining to peep through the yard. I saw a big stone and I grab it up one time.

"Come closer, come closer and see if I won't kill one of allu mother so and so!"

I was serious. One more step from any of them and I was going to pelt the big stone—who it hit it hit, and who get damage, get damage.

"Michelle." I turned around to see Grandma in the road. She was standing there with cousin Grace and the rest ah people that gathered as if somebody died.

"What?"

"Who you talking to so?"

"But Michelle ent have no respect Lou, look how Michelle getting on, and she father right they and look how Michelle talking to you."

Grandma hang she head in shame and she tapped her hands on her leg.

"Ah doh know why this son of mines din leave trouble wey he see it."

I felt the anger running through me again. What the ass was I hearing; did I ask this man to come in his place? I was going, so why the ass he come and take me back?

"Grandma just let me have respect for you, and you Grace, you see how you done old and bend up ah ready. Let me have respect for you too."

Daddy was just standing up in the veranda looking down on me and Mom standing next to him trying to control Chris. I wished she could just let him go so he could do his worse and let me damage him.

"Allu need to call the police. This kind of behaviour is not acceptable and Michelle threatening to burn the house too." Grandma said.

"Yes, let anybody rest they hand on me and see if I ent burning it down to the ground nah, think is joke ah making!"

"Mammy, is trouble ah doh want to get myself in for Michelle. You see I stand up here quiet, quiet you kno, because if I do put me hand on that child is straight Grenada they sending me in the morning. The police now done talk to the little girl, now, now done talk to her and look at she behaviour?" Daddy replied.

"Well call them back. You can't have her disrespecting us like that."

I looked at Grandma and I ent even know what stopping me from telling her bad words.

"Call them police if allu want. Allu feel ah fraid them, or I fraid cell? Ah sure the cell better to sleep in than to be in that stink house with ah set ah nasty people. So call them, I ent care!"

Daddy took out he phone, dialled the police and I heard him talking to an officer.

"I need somebody to come down here now, because this little girl go put me in trouble."

I sat down on the concrete on the edge ah the road, listening to Daddy and I waiting patiently for them police to come. What, they feel ah fraid police? Steups.

"Let them come; you lucky you ent have to call La Qua too."

"Michelle stop it!" Grandma called with tears in her eyes.

"You feel you doing something good? You embarrassing yourself and your father."

"Ah doh care. Who want to be embarrassed let them be embarrassed."

I heard the police vehicle speeding up the hill and I saw the red light as soon as they bent the corner.They pulled up the handbrake by the shop and the vehicle made a screeching sound.

I was still sitting on the piece a wall in the drain. Ah decided I not going nowhere because I ent fraid ah them police.

My phone rang and the little Nokia lighted up.

"Hello?"

"Sabrena wey you?"

"Mama, I did not come again. That stupid man come and take me down from the boat."

"But why? Ah thought he ent want you in his place. Girl leave the people place and come home. You mother house ent leaking and I'll get you back in GSS. I just have to talk to the principal." Ah told Mama ah go call her back and I hung up the phone.

The van pulled up right in front the house; the light shining bright, bright in my eyes as if they want to blind me and deh don't know how to dim it.

"What going on here?" The policeman looked at me sitting on the side of the road, my hands below my chin and I stomping my foot on the ground the same way I does stomp dem when I killing ants.

"You see anything going on here?" I mumbled below my breath, the same way I does mumble when I vex but I ent want nobody hear me.

"What you saying young lady?" he asked with his hands rubbing against the holder of his baton as if he wants to frighten me.

"Thanks for coming." Mom interjected, taking away the attention from the police and me.

"Michelle keeps acting up and I just came from the police station with her. She just cursing and fighting with everybody."

"Oh ho?" I jumped up from the wall and dust my skirt.

"So I just staying just so and curse and fight with people ent? Why you doh tell the police why I cursing and fighting? Why you don't tell the police the trouble allu making me see?"

Grandma watched me below she eyes and I know she meant to shut up, but to hell with Grandma. If she wanted me to shut up then she had to come and shut me up herself.

"All you think because people dey in allu place allu could make them see trouble; allu could tell people what allu want and do what allu want and I should just soak it in; I ent no sponge."

"Aye, aye shut up before I throw you inside the police van and lock you up!" the officer said. I look at him with he belly sticking out of he shirt and I wonder wey the government pick up that "kicksy" police. He looking like a fat boy in a spandex and he telling me about throwing me in the police van. Why he ent throw he self inside they and try to lose some weight, with he fat "ubzerky" self?

"You feel I fraid? You could throw me inside they if you want, anything for me to get out ah them people place; it go make me happy, even if it mean sleeping in the cell. I ent the first and I sure won't be the last."

"So Michelle you ent even have respect for the police eh; is no respect you ent have at all ent?" Daddy said angrily.

I just looked away from him and watched down the road, just in time to catch ah shooting star falling from the sky. I closed me eyes and I made a wish and I know if Daddy did only hear the wish I made he was going to disown and ridicule me one time. When I opened my eyes the star had already faded and I prayed that God, the great God that I serve, was going to listen to my supplication and answer my prayers.

"Come nah pally, come, come. Let's pull this child aside and talk to her because the next phone call I get is lock ah go lock her up in truth. Let she disrespect allu but you see when it comes to me, I ent playing, I don't make joke with my work."

I was tempted to laugh out loud. What joke he was talking bout? Even if he wanted to joke, his face was never going to allow him because he looked as if he bit ah dynamite or he knocked he face against the devil's padlock. Is all my courage I had to master to look at him. So what joke in God's earth he was talking about?

Daddy walked down the step and Mom had she eyes on him as though she counting his every step.

"Baby, don't do nothing stupid you know."

Daddy looked at her. He ent say a word. He just look at her and his expression alone was saying he had everything under control. Daddy reached close to me and ah move my body because I don't want him to touch or even rush me.

"Let's go to the vehicle, and you Miss Lady follow me."

I got up and walked behind them, dragging me foot and making noise with my slippers. We reach where the vehicle was parked up close to the basketball pole; the engine still running and the vehicle dirty.

The policeman looked at me, then he looked at Daddy. He big lips looked like it too heavy for he mouth and I still wondering in me mind how one man could be so ugly. Is like he took ugliness for his whole family, plus for the whole ah the Royal Grenada Police Force.

"I won't be coming back here for a second time eh, and if I have to come back here, I will go with this young lady. I ent just putting her in the cell you kno, ah bringing her in the court and send her straight down with Osprey in the jail tomorrow evening. What wrong with them children these days, you have a good home, a family who loves you and you behaving so? What more you want?"

Family who love me what? I trying me best to keep me mouth shut and not say anything to anybody.

Daddy shook he head,

"Ah really don't know what is wrong with them children in truth, ah really doh know."

I crossed up me eyes and I looked at Daddy with he big hyprocrite self, talking ah set ah shit in me ears.

"So what to do with her?" The policeman asked.

"Just give her one more chance," Daddy replied.

The policeman looked at me and he shook he head - he big bald head that full ah tyres.

"Go inside and behave yourself and don't let me have the chance to come back down here because honestly to God, if I come back you won't like it."

I turned my back and I walked towards the house. I was still dragging my slippers. The dirty dog barked and I wish I had a big stone to open he skull.

I passed Grandma and her "posse" in the road. I ent say ah word to any of them. I just jumped the piece ah wall and walked up the step.

Mom watched me as if to say: *What Daddy make she come back here for*? I ent pay her no mind. I just closed the door and walked inside my room. I bolt the lock behind me and jumped and laid down on me back, looking up in the dark roof, wondering what was really happening in my life. What kind of curse was I facing?

I looked up in the roof and asked myself all kind of questions. Why it is nobody like me? Why people does pretend to care? What I really do Daddy to deserve that kind of cold treatment?

Rain had started falling and the rain drops were hitting the roof creating a song—a song that was forcing my eyes to sleep and taking me slowly away to dreamland.

I had always loved the rain. It's hard to explain but whenever rain starts falling I feel this rather close connection with nature. My heart will skip and I will forget all my sadness and be happy. With each drop of rain, I became happier. Rain always had a way of reminding me of the happy moments of my life—the times we played games under the naked sky as the water soaked our clothes and bathed us at the same time; the times we went under the galvanise and let the water fall in our hair washing out the shampoo that will sometimes burn our eyes; the times we would sit on the river bank and watched as the rain fell making the water dirty; how it ran heavy and how the heavy logs washed down the river banks; the times I would run and play in the mud and it will cling to my skin(the same way it clung to my skin when I got burn from the candle wax); the days we were punished, because we allowed our clothes to get wet from the downpour instead of going somewhere to shelter.

I pulled the cover closer and I shut my eyes as I listened to the lovely raindrops falling heavily on the roof. I could not tell when I fell asleep, but I got up in the morning to the sweet sweet songs of the birds and the crowing of them good for nothing fowls.

Sunlight peeped through the curtains as if it wanting to blind my eyes and I turned my head in the next direction. Last night's activities were still fresh on my mind. But thank God it was Saturday, which meant that I could have just stayed in my room as long as I wanted to without facing anyone. I remained lying down thinking of what it is I would say to Daddy when we came into contact with each other; apologising was out of the question. It was something I found rather difficult to do don't matter how hard I tried. The best solution for now was to avoid everyone, but the question was for how long. We were all living under the same roof, sharing the same convenience, plus Monday was not far away and Daddy had to give me money for school.

I pick up my phone and unlocked the screen and sure enough I had some messages—messages from the boy I was secretly dating.

Chapter 51: Being In Love

Tall, black, muscular and handsome, with long braided hair and a nose as

straight as a ninety degree angle, his legs were long, but he had broad

shoulders to compliment them. I normally teased him about a girl in my class

he once dated and I had no idea when it is I started falling in love with him.

Whenever I see him I will call the girl's name and we will both laugh; his nice white teeth revealing his sweet dimples. He would sometimes say I'm not easy and I will continue making fun of him.

We had exchanged numbers and he made it his duty to text me every morning, noon and night. Sometimes he sent messages or chocolates with his cousin that was in my class—chocolate I had to share of course. His text messages were short but were always effective and it always warmed my heart. I smiled every time I heard the message tone on my phone, hoping it was him. I felt disappointed when it wasn't. I normally replied and within seconds he would send another message to me, letting me know how special I was to him and how much he loved me. He sometimes sent me poems too and he sang songs that always warmed my heart.

Our relationship was a secret because I was too shy to let anyone find out. Besides, I wanted to keep everything on a down low so Daddy won't know.

Our relationship was not sexual and never for the two months we were dating did he pass his place. We would often meet up on Paradise beach, where we had brief conversations with each other—conversations we had to finish on the phone of course because we were trying our best to not make people suspect we were dating each other.

I looked at my phone and smiled. The notification from the message had his name.

Good morning sweedy. I tried calling you last night but somehow I did not get through. Hope all is well and you have a bless day. Love you dearly.

I smiled as I hit the reply button and my heart danced with joy.

Hmm, boy last night was just a crazy night. You remember from the last time what I told you about my brother? Well we had a fall out and I have no idea what he told Daddy, but since after that, Daddy had being acting rather funny. He asked that I leave his place and I did; I should have told you but I tried going back to Grenada.

I had room for just two more characters so I sent the message and started writing all over again.

He came on the boat and there was an uproar. I even ended up in the police tation. Last night we had a falling out again, but the thing is I don't really think Daddy wants me in his place. I just wished I had somewhere else to go. I feel so worthless. I just wish I can die.

Beep, beep, beep

Don't speak like that princess; there is a reason why you are alive; nothing is worth dying for. You will be faced with trials and temptations but you have to be strong and find a way to overcome.

If only it was possible to believe his words! For how long was I going to fight. Was I the best soldier?

Okay I hear you.

Will you like to meet up later?

Later, I can try. You know how difficult it is for me to leave the house especially now with all that drama. I'm not promising you anything but I shall see. I'll text you back and let you know. Please send some credit on my phone. Love you.

Love you too princess and I'll do that as soon as I go down the road.

I looked at his message all over again and tucked the phone below the pillow.

My mind still occupied with all the stupidness happening and I'm feeling as if I'm the most unlucky person in the world. Just when I thought I had escaped from trouble, just when I thought my worries was over, bloody hell, it had only just began, but I was not alone this time; I had a boyfriend who loved me and I loved him just the same.

I found myself wishing I was old enough to make my own decisions. The time felt as if it was creeping by. I wanted to be on my own although it felt like I was already on my own. Well I was on my own having food, shelter and clothing on my back but that was nothing compared to the loneliness my soul felt. It was a loneliness I was willing to trade all the clothes, food, money and privileges to have; a loneliness that made me feel so empty, useless, broken, weak and frustrated; a loneliness I hoped and prayed will go away; It was a hunger I had forever longed to be satisfied, but so far I was still living in that moment and not a thing had changed, nothing what so ever.

Chapter 52: The Aftermath

I heard my cousin's voice from my room. She was just in a higher form than

me but she acted as if she was a big woman. She normally came across when

Daddy was not at home and would gossip with Mom, talking about

everybody's business.

"Mama, what happened here last night; ah hear you and you daughter and them quarrelling?"

"My daughter? Two daughters I have—one here and the other one in America. You mean that thing my husband brought to join our household?"

"Woii allu doh easy nah, but what happen in truth?"

"Girl, the girl in she room."

"Nah she sleeping man, all this action from last night she must be tired."

"Well me ent have time; ah ent know why he bring she here for in the first place. He damn wrong. Ah ent taking part. Anyway, watch how she go have to leave the house by force."

"Ah find so, but why she behaving like that and then walking the road as if she innocent and butter can't melt in she mouth? Is to see her in school always stick up under them teachers and playing Miss Intelligent."

"Girl that's not me business what you tell me. You ent have nothing better to talk about?"

"You going Coconut later?" I often wonder if that girl was a child or a big woman, because all wey drum beat she dey and she so small. If she got lost in a crowd you have to take search light and find her.

I got up from me bed and I walked out the door towards the living room. Dedra was sitting down on the armrest and Mom was on the small chair in the corner by the sofa with her towel wrapped around her and her hair peeping out under she arm as if it looking for breeze.

They both opened they mouth and looked at me as if they saw a ghost. I passed straight without even saying good morning and walked through the kitchen while the bead curtain dancing, creating its own music. I then walked out the back door. Outside was still wet from the heavy showers and water was dripping from the leaves of the tree. Bruno jumped on my legs. I petted her head and she barked at me. She wagged her tail and opened her mouth as if she was about to catch a fly. She jumped on my legs again and I rubbed her fur playfully.

"Be a good dog."

She barked again as if answering and I cut through the short cut behind the house, burst out in front of the shop that grand aunty in America gave my cousin to operate. I looked around for a while. Not a soul in the road. I walked towards the beach and not a soul I saw in the track either. I made my way towards one of the small boats. Using my hands, I rubbed off the water that had settled from the rain and I sat down looking straight into the ocean as the waves splashed on the shore, gathering the leaves and broken branches that were in their way, and pulling them into the depths of the sea.

Chapter 53: Abandoned Again

I returned home just after midday after spending mostly the whole morning

on the beach, doing nothing in particular. I walked back in the house and not

a soul asked me a question. I took my shower, changed my clothes and went

back in my bed. I had no appetite to eat so I was not really thinking about

food - to hell with them and that.

"Michelle come out here at once!" I listened to Daddy's voice summoning me to the living room. I opened the door for the third time and walked out. Everybody was there and Daddy was sitting on the big chair wey up in the corner of the room; his hand resting against the partition. I looked at the pictures on the board to avoid looking at anybody. It had a picture with Daddy kissing Mom on their wedding day. Mom face looked young and she was smiling.

"Well, I'll be leaving for the sea. I might spend more than a year, maybe two years for the most."

Two years? What Daddy was talking about? I felt my heart sink. Why was Daddy going and leave me with these monsters? Yes we fell out lately but Daddy was ten times better than his wife and his children. I had no problem clashing with them, but he was going and leave me here with them? My ears had to be deceiving me.

"Now I have a few expectations whilst I'm out there. I'm going out there to make the best not for myself but for us."

I put me hand below me chin as if I propping sorrow and looked at him straight in he brown eyes. I wanted to lift the world off my shoulder but it was too heavy, so I just continued with my stare and I not blinking. I thinking about what go become of me because the people done ent like me ah ready.

"Michelle, I need you to change you ways and start living in unity. Stop thinking you bigger than everybody and nobody can't correct you. You are a child so I expect you to behave as such, as the Bible says: *When I was a child I act like a child.*"

Sometimes I does wonder if Daddy can't speak without using Scriptures.

"You have to be obedient; we are one family, we live under and we share the same roof. Let us stop behaving as if we is beast. If we can't love who we live with, who else we gonna love? Leave the hooligan behaviour you had in Grenada, in Grenada. If you want to reach far you have to get rid of that ignorance and temper. If you can't do it for me, at least do it for yourself."

I listened to Daddy, not like how I does listen to Miss Blake in Spanish class—the word does pass from one ears and go out the other. But its different now. I taking in every single word that coming out from his mouth. I feeling to cry, but I don't want to put tears in front; I don't want Mom and them to see I weak.

Daddy turned to face Mom—she scratching the weave in her head.

"My wife, I expect you to be a mother to all the children. I know Michelle is not your biological child but you must be a mother to her too. She needs love and I expect you to show her love."

Mom shook she head as if she weak and she body ent have blood—not like the way she does fling it back when she gossiping with her friends.

"Chris, I expect ya'll to behave too; don't give Mom trouble and treat Michelle the way allu will want other people to treat allu."

"When you going?" I asked. I still don't want to believe he was going in truth.

"In two weeks time, might be before."

"Hmmmm." I did not realise I stuepsed and I did not know when it came out. Mom looked at Daddy in a kind ah way as if to say: *That dirty little girl.*

Chapter 54: Back Again

One month ent gone good yet since Daddy gone and me and them fall out

already. I was eventually asked to leave so I had no other option than to pack

me georgie bundle and returned to Grenada—the place I dreaded so much;

the place that reminded me of all the darkness there was in my life.

Mama she self was another case after begging me to come back, ah had to go through all kind of crosses with her. What broke my heart the most was knowing I had to drop out of school, because of me being homeless and Daddy people asking me to leave. But what more could I have done? Mama told me if I waiting for she to get a whore like me in school I go wait long. Mama say she won't waste she precious money on me; she rather throw it down in the latrine hole let worms make feast with it.

So I out of school and most times I just home looking after me brothers and sisters because it ent have nothing really for me to do. Uncle Jack still in prison so is just we and Mama and she still trying to get me to write the letter to say ah lying. I still refused because I can't go back on my words. I can't afford to waste the court's time.

I look at my mother as she bent down sweeping the yard with the bush broom we does cut under the cocoa. Each sweep she made you could hear ah shuffling noise. Mama sweeping but you could see she mind far; I think she thinking about she waste man. She looked up and our eyes met so I turned my head and. looked under the cocoa. I stared at the mango tree. Mango was coming into season.

"Go and get ah cigarette for me Sabrena and bring the matches too."

I got up from where I was sitting on the step—the piece ah board warm, warm as if the sun setting below me. That step is plenty stress and drama, you does have to be very careful how you walking on it because it not too strong. I took some rather big strides and opened the door but I opened it ah little to hard. It knocked against the table in the hall and I prayed in my mind that nothing fell down and broke.

"You want to mash up you father eh Sabrena; you think you could buy a door?"

I pretended not to hear her. I continued to walk towards the shelf wey she does have her cigarettes. Mama have all kind ah thing in that shelf - anything you could think about. She have vicks, sulphur, soft candle, etc. I sure if I dig carefully ah getting kerosene too; fuss Mama have things there. I picked up the box of Special and I looked at the writing on the box: *Smoking is dangerous for your health*. Ah really doh know if she does read that because the woman love she cigarettes, she love it bad, bad. If is one person Mama does make rich is Mr Brown, because she last dollar does go in his pocket. I looked for the matches and I found it, pick it up fast, fast and walked out the door because I don't want Mama to bawl out me name.

"Look Mama, here, it have three more remaining in the pack."

"Three?"

Mama took the cigarettes from me and she scratched the matches. It made a noise then it catch. Then Mama made a big puff and when she blew, smoke came out from she nose and her mouth. That smoke does always make me sneeze—probably it is because of the asthma. But today I ent sneeze; I just stood there looking at Mama as she took another puff. Mama looked more relaxed now; it ent look as if she mind far again.

"Mama, when you going in GSS so that I can go back to school?" I can't even count how many times I asked her that, because I just can't take no for an answer. Mama looked up at me, she smoking she cigarette still, but all the happiness I see in she face vanished.

"Sabrena, stop making you head hard. Ah done tell you ah not spending me money for you to go school; forget about school."

I looked at Mama and it's kinda hard for me to believe what me ears really telling me. Mama is the one that told me to come back in Grenada. She is the one that told me she will talk to Miss Glenda to take me back. CXC was just around the corner. How Mama mean she not sending me in school?

"But Mama, ah doh understand. Is you tell me come back; you ent expect me to drop ah school like that."

"Miss, you better don't fret me mother ass you know" Mama voice changed and she stretched she mouth long as George Degans corner.

"Ah not wasting me money on you ah say; let you man and them send you to school!"

Ah dey and I wondering what man she alking about. My heart sank because I can't believe that's the end of my educational journey. Why Mama asked me to come back if she knew she not sending me to school? Yes things were bad In Carriacou, but at least I would of fight to finish. If I knew Mama's plan was just to have me back in Grenada to make sure I ent progress in life, I would have stayed and grind it. I felt the tears coming, but before I could hide it, Mama saw them and she face flared up in ah rage. Mama began shouting at me just as before.

"Dirty black ugly whore, you get something to cry? Ah tell you ah not sending you to school with my money and that is final! You expect me to send you to school and you have my husband locked up in jail, eh dirtiness? Not ah million like you go get me to send you to school, and come out in front me before I knock you down!"

I look at Mama; the tears still flowing down my cheeks and I wondered wey she get she wickedness from; ah wondering why she so evil. So her plan was really not to see me make it in life, and stupid me fell for her trap.

Chapter 55: Mama's Wrath

"Sabrena, come and take out you stinking, dirty clothes from me bucket!"

I was under the cocoa seated down below the booyee tree, close to Grandpa's grave and I hearing Mama voice loud, loud, loud. They say it ent good to be sitting down in a cemetery but I know Grandpa won't do me anything so I ent fraid.

"Sabrena come and take out you clothes before I throw it down the latrine hole. You buy me blasted bucket!"

I now put me clothes to soak so I ent know what Mama getting on so for. It didn't matter what I do lately—she keep having a problem. If I lay down on the bed she asking me to get up; if I read she find I reading too much; if I ask for more food, she saying I greedy. Ah doh know how to please Mama so I does just go under the cocoa and sit down so I don't have to be close to her. Sometimes I does pray to get big so that I could move out of she house and not go through all this embarrassment and wickedness. I really doh know why ah come back for in the first place. I does wonder why Mama does not treat Elisa and them like that. Yes she does curse them but she does treat me worse.

"Sabrena you doh hear I calling you?!"

I remained under the tree. I really don't have the time for Mama especially on a day like today. She done beat me about ten times for the day ah ready and for nothing. I does wonder why she so wicked and why she treating me like that. Imagine Mama does tell me all kinda thing. She say I bad like soap seed and is only man I good to take. Poor me. When Mama tell me them kind ah thing I does cry. Why she putting bad mouth on me? I don't know.

"Sabrena, if I have to call you again ah bet you, you go meet you dirty clothes and dem outside. You think I is your blasted little girl here eh?"

I got up from the mango stump, dust out me skirt—ah really don't know what I dusting because the way the skirt dirty it can't dirty more than that. I pushed the hoola- hoop slipper in me foot and cut through the track close to Grandpa's grave wey Troy planted some tomatoes that just started to look like it making young ones. I passed below the big starch mango tree that seems to always be in season, then I cut below the nutmeg tree and burst out behind the house close to the latrine. It smelled as if you buried somebody inside it.

I saw Mama from a distance; she bent down scrubbing clothes in the Coppa close to the big stone wey we does hide to bathe. The Coppa is a very big iron basin that we does use to wash, bathe and store water. I heard people say that the Coppa is what they used during slavery to process cane and make sugar. Mama said the museum in town want the Coppa to buy but she not selling it. I was kinda shocked when I heard her say that the first time because other than cigarettes, Mama loves money.

Mama was wearing an old blue skirt and she hair loose up in she head; she black jersey have a big rip in the side and she was scrubbing the clothes hard, hard. I could hear the scrubbing brush from quite behind the house. Me clothes were in the white bucket we got in Mr Cuth's shop—the bucket that he took out the pig tail from and throw outside, and Mama begged him for it. The bucket was close to Mama. I was afraid to go and take it out because I didn't want her to hit me.

Mama looked up and saw me and she stood up straight, straight. The sun was hitting she face the same way It does hit the cashew nut when we put it to dry. Mama ent even blinking; she just starring at me with she mouth long like to-to-mel-pan-cup.

"Sabrina, so you have to please you self before you could come eh, you doh hear how long I calling you?"

Ah didn't answer because I ent want to say the wrong thing to provoke Mama's wrath. Ah doh want the wrong words to jump out me mouth like how it jumped out the other day when she called me a football and I told her what she have to know she ent know it. I really don't want to say anything so I just started walking towards the Coppa, towards Mama and me heart beating fast fast like them drums them man does be beating when it have Saracca.

"So you ignoring blasted me? Like you doh hear I talking to you. When I talk to you answer me! Answer fucking me!"

"But Mama I was under the cocoa."

What you doing under the cocoa? So because you under the cocoa you can't answer me?"

"I was coming, Mama, I was walking up."

"Doh Mamma me you know, me is not you blasted mother; ah tired tell you that. Why you doh take you fucking clothes and go under the cocoa and stay? Take all you clothes and go down they!"

I stood looking at Mama and I trying to force me self from crying, but me eyes heavy as if it had gravel in them. As I tried to keep it in, it fell down me face. I raised me hand quick, quick like lightening to wipe it but Mama saw it too.

"You, this little Jezebel, you always quick to put tears in front. Ah tired tell you is wicked people that always quick to cry. If you want something to cry ah go give you! Elisa go and get a cacolie whip for me." I was about to run but Mama grabbed me by me collar. I fought to get away but she grabbed me tighter.

"Mama. No, no, no, Mama, no!"

"Hush you stinking cunt. Is something you want to cry so ah go give you!"

I felt me heart sank. If is one thing, Mama does beat real bad. When she beating you is like she does not want to stop and me skin done full ah bruisse and bobo ah ready. I look at Elisa walking down the steps.

"Hurry up Elisa, ah go teach this little dirtiness ah lesson."

Elisa cut through the track and ah praying she come back with a small whip, but when Elisa came back my heart sank because it was ah big, big cacolie whip. It big like them piece ah spice wood we does cut and scrape under the cocoa. And the darn stupid girl take out all the leaves and she plait the little loose pieces the same way she does plait me hair, neat, neat! For the first time in my life I wish Elisa coulda just fall down and dead. Why she had to follow Mama instructions? Why she had to go and get this big whip?

"Hurry up before I cut you ass too!" Elisa walked fast, fast. She bow legs moving like if she is one of them stupidee children. Mama grabbed the whip from Elisa and the next thing I felt was the burning pain on my back, cutting deep, deep down in me skin. With each blow I was dancing, trying to soothe the pain but my efforts were meaningless; it stung my back the same way that worthless man used to sting my vagina.

"Oh gawd! Oh gawd!" I screamed.

"Hush you stinking mouth, before I kill you."

"Ah go call the police! Ah go call the police!"

"Oh so you want to call the police?" Mama pushed me hard and I knocked me head on the post below the house—the post the people from Red Cross put up when they were building the house. I cried in pain again, and this time Mama pushed me down on the ground. She took she foot and put it right in me throat. Ah ent have no more strength to cry so I just close me eyes hoping I will just take my last breath and die. Ah tired ah every blasted thing.

"Call the police when I done kill you. You feel you go make them lock me up the same way you make them lock up me husband?"

Chapter 56: Mind Made Up

I made up my mind. If saying I lied was going to get Uncle Jack out of jail

and give me the opportunity to go to school then I might as well do it. After

all I don't want my education to go down the drain; I had big dreams and I

had plans for the future too. I don't want no outside latrine; I want a house

with bathroom and toilet. I don't want nobody hand it down to me; I want to

build it myself, and so my only hope is education. I tied me head with a rag and I walked outside. Mama was sitting down on the bucket killing ants. She

does dig the ants nest, put a white diaper on the nest, let all them ants gather

and she will sit down and kill them. I does wonder if them stinging ants ent

biting Mama because I never see nobody do that before.

"Mama." I walked towards her while she was crushing the small ants between she two big thumbs.

"What is it again Sabrena, you can't give me ah rest?"

"Mama ah go say I lied. Ah go make Uncle Jack come out ah jail." She dropped the diaper with the ants and she look at me —pale, pale, pale as if she just saw she dead father and she can't believe her eyes.

"You sure girl, you know what you saying?"

"Yes ah go do it. Just tell me what to say and take me by the person I have to tell and I will make him come out."

It was not what I really wanted but it was what's best for me at the moment. I had lost too much and I did not want to lose my education too— my education was the most valuable thing to me so if I had to get it instead of justice then fine, because Uncle Jack had done desecrate me ah ready. That was the past but finishing school was the future and I had to finish at all cost.

Mama looked at me and leaned forward to make sure she was hearing what I was saying.

"Sabrena you sure?"

"Yes ah sure, just tell me what you want me to say and I'll say it." Ah really don't like how me and Mama living either. I want her to play a motherly role in my life. I want to know how it feels to be loved by her and most of all I want to end the bickering and name calling. I was willing to do anything for peace.

Mama gave a big smile. All of a sudden she got happy.

"Let's go inside Sabri."

Mama got up and I followed her. She walked in she room, dust out she foot on the piece ah cloth by she bed and lay down on the mattress. I stood while leaning me body against the partition. I didn't really want to sit down; I just wanted her to tell me what to do and I will do it.

Well Mama had she hands below she chin—the same way it does be when she eating and lay down.

"You will have to write a letter. When you write that letter I will take it to the lawyer and we will all sign."

"We all? What you mean, we all?"

"Well me, you and the lawyer and whosoever else will be a witness Sabrena."

"That's all?"

"Well maybe we might have to go to the JP, but that will be determined by the lawyer. We can go by she office tomorrow; it done late ah ready."

"Oh ok, then maybe I should start writing the letter."

"No, wait until we go by the lawyer. You can always write it at her office."

"That's all?"

"Yes."

"Oh ok. Well I going under the cocoa and see if I get any cashew."

Mama shook she head at me and I walked out the room door with a heavy heart. What a mother! She was going all out to protect her husband and get him out of jail, even if it meant using me as the bait, and she was not even considering sending me back to school. Her own child she carried for nine months in pain and discomfort; the child she had to bawl 'oh god, oh god nurse' to push out. What a woman! What a life! What a mother!

The following morning bright and early we made our way to the lawyer's office. We met my big sister Dedra at the St David's bus stand and we all walked across to Scotiabank, where we had to climb the stairs to get to the office. Although there were plenty stairs to climb, the view was breathtaking and all that was on my mind was to get this 'comess' done and over with. Going back on my words was going to be rather difficult, but I had to do it.

Mama walked in the office with she perspiration bag stuck below her arm and her shoes making loud, loud noise on the people tiles. Dedra followed. No one was saying much. We were mostly quiet.

"Dedra which part we going?" I tugged at her pants and she looked back at me.

"Right in the office inside dey," she replied.

The glass door had the sign *Open* and Mama walked right in. She was greeted by an Indian lady on the desk that my sister later indicated was the lawyer's sister. After Mama told her the reason why we there, she asked that we have a seat. There was

enough chairs for everybody. I sat in the chair closer to the door and rubbed my hands together because the AC was cold. Dedra sat right next to me and Mama occupied the seat in the corner. I gazed around the room not looking at anything but trying to keep my mind occupied and not think of what I was about to do. I glanced at Mama and she had a glow on her face; the anger had diminished somewhat and she was looking more relaxed. I shook my head in disbelief and looked around just in time to see Dedra staring at me. Our eyes made four corners and she looked away. I looked away too, avoiding any further eye contact with her.

About ten minutes later we were joined by the lawyer. She asked that we follow her to the office. I had an instant headache the minute I laid my eyes on her. Everything from the court case came rushing back at me, causing a great commotion in my mind. She was the one who called me a liar, saying I was lying on my stepfather and here I was to prove her words true. Was I really a liar? At that moment I surely felt like one. The question as to where Mama was getting money to pay her lawyer fees had crossed my mind. Was Mama pulling the devil's tail because it was only obvious that she had no money since she was now struggling twice as hard to make ends meet?

We followed her. I was trailing behind like a turtle because all of a sudden I felt a weight on my feet.

"So why are you here?" she asked Mama, not even waiting for us to settle down.

"Well Sabrena is here to let you know that she was telling a lie."

She looked at me and I felt embarrassed. I glanced at the window and into the blue seas. A fishing boat sped across leaving a white trail behind.

"Hmm," she said, "So she finally have a conscience huh?" She was not looking at me. She was pulling out the draw on her desk as if she was looking at something. I kept quiet with eyes still fixed on the ocean, glancing around every now and again.

"So let's hear what you have to say Miss Sabrena."

I wondered why she was addressing me as Miss. I was feeling the same way I felt at the court room—depressed and broken. I remained quiet; my tongue was heavy all of a sudden and I was finding it difficult to open my own mouth.

"Sabrena is you the lady talking to."

"No Mama, leave her; she thinks people have time to waste."

I looked at Dedra and wondered why she was opening she mouth; why did Mama invited her in the first place? I then realised the stupid question I was asking myself. Dedra was her support system because all of them had joined together and called me a liar and even went out of their way to make my life a living hell—calling my school to say I was a liar amongst other hurtful and intimidating things.

"I will like to let you know I'm lying. Uncle Jack did not do anything to me; everything was a made up story." My words were choking me. What was I really doing?

"And it took you all this while to say that?"

"Yes"

"But why did you tell such an expensive lie, a lie that has my client behind bars for a crime he did not commit?" I cursed myself in my mind and my belly dropped. Crime he did not commit me big toe.

"Because I felt like it."

"You felt like it!" She was now raising her voice and both Mama and Dedra stood there looking on without saying a word.

"Yes I felt like it, and now I'm telling you the truth."

"So you think this is funny right? You lied on your stepfather because you felt like it? You know how serious is the accusation of rape? Did you for once sit yourself down and think about the consequences before making such accusation? Did you think about all the things you put your family through, especially you mother?"

"Eh huh."

"Eh huh? Don't address me like that!"

I was fuming.

She then asked Mama to take me to the DPP where I could relate exactly what it is I was saying to her.

As I walked out the office I felt as if I was hurting myself. There was no way I was going to continue with the lies. I could not change my story. I was going to tell the DPP the truth. I related everything to the DPP. Mama was upset but I could not care less. Uncle jack had raped me continuously; he had taken away my pride and innocence, and robbed me off my childhood.

Chapter 57: Deceived Again

"Cokey o' ko." Today is a holiday. Ah hate it when them cocks crow. I turned on me mattress and let go one big stupse. Ah know if Mama only hear me she bursting me mouth. They does make some loud, loud noise as if people killing them. They does choose to crow when people just start to enjoy sleep. Sometimes I does just want to hold them and beat out all their feathers. Like they ent know how to enjoy sleep. As six o'clock comes they does climb on Miss Ann tree and go to sleep and nobody don't disturb them you kno, but yet they can't allow you sleep in peace. I pulled the sheet over me head and put me hands over me ears.

I really not in the mood for them stupid birds this morning and I just hope they could keep quiet. When is not them is Mama—she waking up early, early in the morning and making a set ah noise. Either she cursing about the clothes Troy have in the bucket soaking for days, or the dreevay he dreevaying. Like she herself ent know what its like to sleep in her bed. Ah never meet up a woman that 'fraid her bed and could talk so. Ah can't hate that stupidness more than I hate it already. Its one thing to get up early but it's another thing to get up and then nobody can sleep.

Mama does normally get up and make bakes early for breakfast. You does know when she making bakes, because she does be cutting the wood hard, hard and dashing them on the galvanise in the kitchen outside, making me heart jump with each bang. Donelle does vex too. She does just turn on the mattress and cover her ears. Sometimes she does look at me and all I could do is shake me head. I wish Mama could just shut she big mouth. Early in the morning she would be singing:

Jean and Dina, Rosita and Clementina,

Round the corner smoking,

Bet you life is something they selling,

And if you catch them broken

You can get them all for nothing,

So doh make ah row,

Yankee gone and Sparrow take over now.

Mama ent no best singer with nice voice but early, early in the morning the woman does be singing away.

I can't sleep anymore so I just got up from the bed, sat down and I leaned my back on the board. I stupsed again knowing very well it ent even six o'clock yet. My mind ran on me flowers and I jumped up from the bed, grabbing up my pants from the dirty clothes heap. I put it on and walked outside wey the morning breeze hit me hard, hard on me face.

"Good morning Mama."

"Morning. Wey you going this hour ah the morning? You brush you teeth?"

"No, no I just going and wet me flowers before the sun comes up—ah coming back now."

I walked towards the gap, kicked a big stone and me toe cried out in pain.

"Sabrena." I turned around just in time to see Mama pulling out the fiber from the coconut shell.

"Yes?"

"Ah want you to watch the children for me; I have to go in the hospital to come back."

I know Mama ent talking about the hospital in Mirebeau; she talking about the one in town. I kinda wondering how she never say anything about hospital before. Why all of a sudden she going in hospital? But she was only human so she was entitled to forget.

"Yes," I answered and walked towards the pipe.

The rest of my day was spent looking after the children and looking through Mama's very important bag because somehow I was not convinced with her hospital story. Although I tried to dismiss it, it was still playing on my mind. I opened the bag and I emptied everything on she mattress, going through each and every piece ah paper in detail. Ah picked up ah paper that looked like a summons and I hoping to myself is not what I thinking. I opened it with trembling hands, reading slowly—the contents fulfilling my fears. I stamped my foot on the floor as anger took over my whole body. Why did ah big woman as Mama lied to me? I sat down on the step waiting patiently for Mama to come back and them children sat down on the step with me too.

I felt a rage as I saw Mama breaking the gap. In a split second the rage turned to fright. Walking behind Mama with his bag and baggages was the monster himself, Uncle Jack!

Glossary

Allu- All of you

Awah- or what

Bam bam- bottom/rear end

Banganet- A rod and knife used to pick fruits.

Basket mouth- Wide mouth/talkative

Bloods- A casual group/gang

Boi- Boy

Boom- Have sex

Buff- fat

Caca- Crap

Campesh- Type of wood

Cawaying- Walking with style

Cock and bull- False story/tale

Cock up- Sitting

Cocojay- Dried tears

Cokey- Cross-eyed

Coks-e-coks- Heels/Stilettos

Cun cun- Female genital

Darling- darling

Doodoo- Darling- A term used to call little children

Dotish- stupid/foolish

Dougla- A person who is mixed with Indian and negro

Drag-a-bat- A wild person

Dreevay- Travel around

Dribble- drop of saliva from one's mouth

Farine- Grounded Cassava

Fass- Inquisitive

Forward- rude

Fuss- Unessecary concern

Gallay- Blemished Skin

Georgie bundle- Load

Grandcharge- Threatening to fight

Hightitity- Rich/wealthy

Jook- Pushing something against someone

Joppa- Old house

Juck- Masturbate

Jumbie- Spirit/Dead Spirit

Ka-ka-jay- Dried tears

Kicksy- hysterical/funny

Kiss-meh-assing- damn

La Diablesse- Legend from Caribbean folklore

Leggo beast- wild animal

Likkle- little

Macco- Often refers to someone who is concerned with people's business

Magga- slim/thin

Mama Malady- Also from Caribbean folklore (but is seen as a woman)

Mess- Foolishness/feces

Nah-No

Ouii- Yes

Oye-Hey/Hello

Pally- Friend

Pappyshow- Foolishness

Pee- urine/urinate

Posse- crew

Pumping up- Gearing up/Energised

Pwel- Pubic hair

Reds- Fairskinned person

Sada- Someone without teeth

Sistah- Sister

Sovet- Crayfish

Steups- A sucking noise made with the tongue pressed against the teeth used to express annoyance or frustration.

Stupidee- Stupid/foolish person

Sush shushing- Hush

Talawa- Strong

Trust- Taking an item at a shop to pay at a later date.

Ubzerky- Big/fat

Wawet- Luck

Yank- Hard pull